DEEP DIVERS

"Shakil Choudhury offers a genuinely new and fresh
and so often *do not see* each other. He offers practical ᴛᴏᴏɪs ror transforming from
an 'Us versus Them' mentality to a mindset that honours and grows our deep
diversity. Meticulously researched and beautifully written in an inviting narrative
style, this is a must-read for anyone concerned with race, difference, and diversity."

> — JAMES ORBINSKI, Head of Mission for Doctors Without Borders
> during Rwandan genocide, author of *An Imperfect Offering:
> Humanitarian Action in the Twenty-first Century*

"Shakil Choudhury has written a breakthrough book about how to achieve the
kind of racial equity that goes far beyond traditional notions of 'diversity.' In his
deep dive, he grapples with the implications of several decades of neuroscience,
reflecting on the role of emotion in racial matters, while still grounded in systems,
rules, and power. Everyone working on race issues should read this book. Even
when you don't agree, you will be provoked to think harder about the enormity
of our challenge, and how to generate the emotional and intellectual fortitude to
meet that challenge."

> — RINKU SEN, Executive Director of Race Forward and publisher of Colorlines

"*Deep Diversity* offers an important analysis to help us achieve the genuine reconciliation that we must achieve between Canadians and Indigenous peoples in
order to move forward."

> — ARTHUR MANUEL, Neskonlith, Secwepemc Nation,
> author of *Unsettling Canada: A National Wake-Up Call*

"Choudhury's text offers straightforward tools that can help everyone assess their
own innate reactions in any situation. More than that, it's a great read—the book
derives its heart from its author, who writes scientifically but very personally,
confronting his own discriminatory reactions unflinchingly, as he asks us to do,
and effortlessly straddling the line between insightful analysis and compelling
narrative."

> — JORDAN HEATH-RAWLINGS, deputy editor, *Sportsnet* magazine

"While reading this wonderful book, I felt alternately humbled, deeply moved, in admiration, grateful, impatient, and profoundly hopeful—sometimes all at once . . . Shakil's willingness to hold his mistakes up for scrutiny and insight invited me to do the same. He matter-of-factly insists that each of us, no matter what body we're in, has a responsibility to heal the racism in ourselves and in the world around us. It's infectious because the book doesn't stop there. Written into every chapter are specific skills we can practice as citizens of the world wanting to live in connection with our neighbours."

— BARB THOMAS, social justice facilitator, writer, and activist, co-author
of *Dancing on Live Embers: Challenging Racism in Organizations*

"*Deep Diversity* is a valuable read for leaders looking to better understand how to successfully lead today's increasingly diverse workplace environments. By combining research findings with his own personal experiences and insights, Shakil Choudhury helps us to understand what's behind our inherent biases and beliefs about those different from us, and what we can do to overcome them in order to create a more inclusive workplace environment and worldview."

— TANVEER NASEER, MSc., award-winning leadership writer,
Inc. 100 leadership speaker, co-author of *Leadership Vertigo*

"As the Associate Director of Canada's second-largest public school board, it has been my pleasure to work closely with Shakil Choudhury and to encourage the introduction of the principles outlined in *Deep Diversity*, which have proven effective in our workplace and classroom equity efforts. I commend his work and recommend this book as an essential resource for equity and inclusion educators everywhere."

— SCOTT MOREASH, Associate Director, Peel District School Board

"I sincerely wish this book had been written ten years ago. I saw myself in many of the experiences and struggles described, as I'm sure many of my equity colleagues will. I was in tears twice reading this—it really got to the core of why this work is so difficult, and why it's so rewarding . . . *Deep Diversity* emphasizes the importance of relationships and compassion, principles I have always maintained are keys to equity work . . . I found this book not only helpful but also hopeful. Miigwetch for sharing this."

— DONNA GERBER, Aboriginal Liaison and Recruitment Manager,
Niagara College

DEEP
DIVERSITY

OVERCOMING US vs. THEM

SHAKIL
CHOUDHURY

BETWEEN THE LINES
TORONTO

Deep Diversity
© 2015 Shakil Choudhury

First published in 2015 by
Between the Lines
401 Richmond Street West
Studio 281
Toronto, Ontario M5V 3A8
Canada
1-800-718-7201
www.btlbooks.com

Library and Archives Canada Cataloguing in Publication

Choudhury, Shakil, author
Deep diversity : overcoming us vs. them / Shakil Choudhury.

Includes bibliographical references and index.
Issued in print and electronic formats.
ISBN 978-1-77113-025-7 (paperback). — ISBN 978-1-77113-026-4
(epub). — ISBN 978-1-77113-027-1 (pdf)

1. Prejudices.   2. Racism—Psychological aspects.   I. Title.

BF575.P9C46 2015   303.3'85   C2015-903799-9
C2015-903800-6

Design: Gordon Robertson
Printed in Canada, eighth printing September 2018

We acknowledge for their financial support of our publishing activities the Government
of Canada through the Canada Book Fund, the Canada Council for the Arts, which last year
invested $153 million to bring the arts to Canadians throughout the country, and the
Government of Ontario through the Ontario Arts Council, the Ontario Book Publishers
Tax Credit program, and the Ontario Media Development Corporation.

To Arion, Koda, and the next generation.
May you build on our successes
and learn from our mistakes.

CONTENTS

PREFACE

HE DEEP DIVERSITY model outlined in this book seeks to reframe the debate regarding systemic racism and discrimination in a practical, scientific, and compassionate manner. It is intimately tied to my personal and professional story. It's a culmination of twenty years in the field of diversity and inclusion, one emotional burnout in my early thirties, and a childhood pretending I was white.

I've had the honour of teaching, working with, and learning from thousands of people and many organizations in North America, Central and South America, Europe, and South Asia. That's provided a lot of grist for the mill on the topic of race, ethnicity, and culture. I've been involved with projects that were substantial successes, fabulous failures, and everything in between.

The Five Approaches to Racial, Ethnic, and Cultural Cohesion sidebar gives a thumbnail sketch of several basic ways to approach the work I do—multiculturalism, cross-cultural communication, business case for diversity, cultural intelligence, and anti-racism. I also offer my perspective on the strengths and weaknesses of each approach. Overall, I see them as strategies to help both individuals and groups nurture environments in which all people feel they matter and belong, with fairness and justice as underlying principles. Essentially, this work strives to increase the sense of "us" while reducing the feelings of "them."

Of the approaches I've listed, the last one, the justice case called anti-racism, is the most challenging and contentious of the bunch. It's also my

FIVE APPROACHES TO RACIAL, ETHNIC, AND CULTURAL COHESION

1. **Multiculturalism:** The sharing of cultural foods and celebrations, including dance, songs, and art. This approach is easy to do, engaging, and fun but pretty laissez-faire about making concrete social change.

2. **Cross-cultural Communication:** This approach focuses on learning about cultural customs, norms, and differences in communications styles to achieve specific goals. For example, Mexicans favour relationship building before getting down to business deals, Asian people don't make eye contact as a sign of respect, and Muslims don't shake hands with members of the opposite sex. These strategies can be helpful to understand certain customs within ethnocultural groups. Frequently, though, they rely on generalizations that are a bit too fixed, reinforcing stereotypes.

3. **Business Case for Diversity:** In the context of an organization, this approach focuses on the bottom-line benefits of a diverse, inclusive workforce. This strategy is beneficial in attracting buy-in by senior decision makers. However, it tends to candy-coat issues of discrimination and racism, usually avoiding the difficult issues.

4. **Cultural Intelligence:** A more recent approach that combines cross-cultural communication with emotional intelligence strategies. It is still emerging and appears to work well for international teams needing to collaborate in global locations. This approach can also reinforce stereotypes nationally and locally, ignoring the role of systemic power and bias.

5. **Anti-racism:** From this perspective, discrimination and racism are systemic; therefore, understanding the dynamics of power and privilege between white and racialized/Aboriginal peoples is essential to creating inclusion. This approach falls under the umbrella of anti-oppression education, which critically examines the dynamics between dominant and non-dominant groups and identifies the redistribution of power as key to making change. Anti-racism and anti-oppression more broadly,

however, frequently shut people down with hard-edged strategies that can feel like "shame and blame."

There are other well-known approaches, such as intercultural communication or cultural proficiency, which many would suggest are unique strategies unto themselves. I would agree, and also argue that although they have important strengths, they are modifications, combinations, or advancements on the above five strategies. For simplicity, I've identified these as starting points.

background. My master's thesis was focused on anti-racist education, helping establish the foundation of my early career. But it is not as dominant as it once was in my life and work. And that's a key part of the backstory of why Deep Diversity came to be.

Anti-racism is a political theory founded on the following premise. Racism can be eliminated, but to do so, power and its abuses must be addressed on both individual and institutional levels. For this to be meaningful, significant emphasis is placed on the change being systemic. As the theory goes, in a society where racism exists, it is not enough to be non-racist. For real transformation to occur, one has to actively challenge discrimination in all its forms. One has to be *anti-racist*.

For a long time, I used this particular worldview exclusively. It helped me make sense of my life as a racialized person, growing up in Canada and struggling with feelings of inferiority. Although I was a popular, high-achieving kid, I grew up trying to hide my South Asian heritage. This experience of shame, I would later learn, is fairly common among "minority" group members. In my desperate bid to fit into a white society, I went so far as to avoid other brown kids. Frequently, I behaved as though and believed that I was white. I also remember feeling a distorted sense of pride if anyone confused me as being Italian or Spanish.

At the time, I didn't have the language to recognize—let alone describe—the feelings of inadequacy that I was wrestling with. It wasn't until my

A TERMINOLOGY NOTE

White refers to those people who trace their ethnic roots historically to the European context.

People who are racial minorities are referred to as *racialized, non-white, person of colour,* or *racial minority.* To keep the book user-friendly I use these terms interchangeably, even though the preferred term today is *racialized.* (For more detail, see Race Is Social, Not Biological in chapter 4.)

Aboriginal, or *Indigenous,* refers to people who identify as First Nations, Métis, Inuit, or Native American. Aboriginal peoples have a unique history as the original inhabitants in the Americas with the right to self-determination and treaty rights. Indigenous communities thus are recognized as distinct from other racial minority groups.

mid-twenties that I started to make sense of my experience using anti-racism and, more broadly, anti-oppression principles. I encountered government reports, commissions, and umpteen studies that clearly demonstrated that racialized and Aboriginal people were treated worse than their white counterparts by so many social measures. (See sidebar: A Terminology Note.) Throughout North America, these measures include access to jobs, pay, health care, education, and fairness in the justice system.

There was even a term to describe my childhood feelings of cultural shame and rejection: *internalized racism.* The quantity and clarity of information was both overwhelming and empowering.

I felt shocked, furious—and transformed—by what I was learning. I was stunned that I had never been taught about systemic discrimination before. The theory meshed with my experiences. It helped make sense of much of my life. I felt very powerful and in control in a personal way that I hadn't previously. Although I didn't know it at the time, this would be my life's work. My identity became that of an anti-racist educator and activist. I took on all the trappings that come with that, including a sense of power and authority, not to mention a touch of born-again fervour.

By the time I was thirty, I'd accomplished a number of things. Some highlights included managing community projects in Costa Rican rainforests, co-ordinating an oral-history project between young leaders in Pakistan and Canada, and spearheading economic/political literacy workshops for local low-income communities in Toronto, my home. I was a founding teacher of an alternative school and had put in countless volunteer hours for community-based organizations around the city. I was also getting accolades for my work as an anti-racist educator, including a provincial award for anti-bias curriculum development.

But things were not all rosy in Activist Land.

There was also a downside to being well versed in anti-racism content and learning processes. I perceived racism, discrimination, and oppression everywhere I went. This became an unconscious habit, an exclusive view on life. (One that was a little gloomy, to say in the least.) We lived on a bleak, unjust planet that was sinking fast. Saving the world was a thankless, never-ending task that also seemed not to be a choice. I felt compelled to do it, and resentful that most of society appeared to be unaware or not care. I prioritized my work and the needs of strangers ahead of time with my loved ones. And they began to wonder why I wasn't around and why I was always so exhausted.

I didn't know it, but I was entering the territory of personal burnout.

I also had an emerging realization that the social justice community I so admired also had its share of power dynamics, toxicity, and egos. In spite of the philosophies of many progressive organizations, we were hardly models of healthy relationships. This made our criticism of corporate or mainstream organizations feel hollow. Our relationships were just as fractured as anyone else's, so our belief systems had little hope of being lived out in their fullness.

I recall one situation that unmoored me, shortly after the 9/11 terrorist attacks in the United States. I watched a group of my activist peers bicker and snipe at each other in a meeting, as they tried to decide how to respond to such an immense tragedy. Various worldviews were competing to influence the room, including anti-war, anti-racism, anti-globalization, anti-poverty, union, direct action, and feminist perspectives. The environment was sharply divided, political, and terribly unfriendly—surprising, considering that these people supposedly held a common vision for a socially just world. The feeling of "us" and "them" was in the room, but we couldn't see it.

Inside, my anger and frustration were boiling over. *This is my community? This is who I look up to and whose affirmation I desire? If we can't keep it together, who can? I do* not *need this!*

I was overstretched as it was. Instead of engaging in the room, I began to detach.

At the same time, in my personal life, things were becoming unbalanced, with many relationships fraying. I was unable to meet my obligations to those I loved most. I felt resentful about giving so much of my time to the outside world, and began to question what I was doing and why. I was worn out and emotionally adrift.

I walked away from community organizing and activism.

In retrospect, burning out was the best thing that could have happened to me. I was forced to embark on a painful journey of healing and self-discovery. Over the next decade, I drew on my middle-class privilege and networks to find supports through friends, mentors, coaches, therapists, and trusted colleagues. I uncovered unhealthy inter- and intrapersonal patterns. I acknowledged old wounds and became more intentional about what I was doing and where I was going.

I began to realize that the dysfunction in my life mostly had to do with me—my choices, actions, and reactions. I began to understand an infuriating yet liberating lesson, one that has been plainly stated by a number of wise elders such as Epictetus and the Dalai Lama. Although we rarely control our circumstances, we always have choice over how we react to them.

The tricky part was starting to uncover the unconscious aspects of what I thought, said, and did that caused me trouble. Over several years, I became more aware. I developed better habits in the choices I made and in managing myself, especially in stressful and charged situations. I felt more in control and more spacious. The feeling of being tossed about by the waves of existence began to recede. And I learned an essential lesson for change makers. To make the world a better place, we also need to tend our inner world, to mend the broken parts we carry within.

My healing journey was a literacy training of sorts. It helped me understand my own emotions and offered insights into otherwise unconscious behaviours and choices. Seeing the value of developing greater self-awareness and self-management skills, I became curious. Why wasn't emotional literacy integrated into the work we were doing, not only in the social change sector, but also in society at large?

I began loosening the attachment to my ideological roots of anti-racism and exploring other avenues of thought. I began to integrate research and strategies from the fields of emotional intelligence, social psychology, neuroscience, implicit bias, and mindfulness. This searching would eventually result in Deep Diversity, a practical, scientific, and compassionate framework to help us deal more effectively with issues of racial difference.

What I've come to understand, and what this book will explore, is that the problems of diversity are not cognitive in nature. There is no shortage of good ideas about how to make people feel like they matter and belong. Our blocks exist at the feeling, unconscious level. When we encounter those who are racially different than us, our unconscious, emotional selves can take over. And yet, most of the approaches used today are very cognitive, or head-based. To undo a problem that is emotional in nature, it is not very effective to try to think our way through it. Like throwing a fire extinguisher to a drowning person, it's the wrong tool for the task.

Deep Diversity seeks to integrate head and heart—feelings and thoughts—in a way that is non-judgmental yet challenging. To overcome the systemic problems of racism and discrimination, we must notice ourselves moment to moment. We must accept our flaws and biases, while recognizing the need to change.

The Deep Diversity framework is not only more effective for the people and organizations I work with, it's also more personally sustainable. It emphasizes relationship building rather than political ideology as the foundation for racial and intergroup harmony. Having taught this framework extensively, I've found that it leaves people curious about themselves and their dynamic with others. This curiosity can reduce the Us versus Them dynamic and expand our sense of "we." Even as it tackles the polarizing and painful issues of racism and discrimination, Deep Diversity is fundamentally hopeful.

In this area, as in others, an optimistic perspective is very important. In the words widely attributed to Holocaust survivor Elie Wiesel: "Hope is like peace. It is not a gift from God. It is a gift only we can give one another."

1

THE FOUR PILLARS
OF DEEP DIVERSITY

What We Say, Not What We Do

A UNIVERSITY STUDENT, Nina, sits patiently in the waiting area of a nondescript office. Two other students, one black and one white, are also waiting to be called in. After a few moments, the black student notices his cell phone is missing and heads to the adjacent hallway to retrieve it. On his way out, he accidentally bumps the white student's leg. No words are exchanged, but once the black student has left the waiting room, the white student mutters: "Clumsy nigger."

Nina[1] has arrived at this office to be part of a research project. She doesn't realize, though, that the study has already begun in the waiting room. What's happening is part of a Canada-U.S. study conducted by researchers from York University, the University of British Columbia, and Yale University.[2] The black and white students are actors, and the focus of the study is on Nina's response.

Subjects were divided into three research groups. One group saw this exchange happen on a video (Watchers). A second group only read about it (Readers). The third group (Experiencers) actually experienced the interaction directly with live black and white actors.

Unsurprisingly, when asked to imagine themselves in this situation, the Readers and Watchers indicated that they would be outraged. When asked which student they would choose to work with in a follow-up activity, more than 80 per cent of the Watchers said that they would choose to work with the black student over the white student. Similarly, about 75 per cent of the Readers said that they, too, would choose the black student as a partner.

None of these results should be surprising. After all, they took place in 2009 in a university setting in Toronto, one of the world's most multicultural cities.

But what were the results from the Experiencers group? How did Nina and others like her respond? How many of the Experiencers said or did anything in response to the racist comment?

We would expect the numbers to be a little bit lower. For most of us, responding in real time is more difficult than an imagined intervention. Maybe 50 per cent of the study group would have stepped in? But perhaps that still sounds too high. A conservative guess might be that 30 per cent— three out of every ten students—would have said or done something in response. Or sceptics in the crowd might suggest that only one out of ten students would step in.

The actual results? According to study co-author Kerry Kawakami, of those who experienced the racist event first-hand, *no one* intervened or said anything.[3] Nor, when interviewed later, did anyone report being upset by the comment. And disturbingly, most of the students chose the white person who made the racist comment as their partner for a later assignment.

Excuse me? Yes—you read that correctly. The vast majority of the students—over 70 per cent—chose the white student rather than the black student as a partner, despite having witnessed the incident first-hand.

Here's another twist—all of the students who participated in the study were non-black. Some were white; some came from a variety of ethnocultural racial backgrounds. They were well educated, young, and living in a profoundly multiracial city. A diverse bunch of university students—the odds don't get much better for a group we would expect to have empathy for their peers and potentially intervene in such a situation.

The researchers concluded that this study is an example of our inability to accurately predict how we will *feel*—and therefore react—in future situations, especially regarding bias and discrimination. The study investigated emotions and behaviours in the context of racial difference.

So why are emotions important? This is the first insight about issues of diversity and inclusion. *How we feel directly influences how we act.*[4]

Our emotions are invisible and controlling. Whether we're aware of them or not, they significantly influence our choices and behaviours. Some scientists even argue that we feel rather than think our way through the world.[5] Further, social pain (for example, being excluded) and physical pain (such as being hit) share overlapping neural regions in the brain. This helps shed light on why angry expressions or words of rejection can hurt so much.[6]

To tackle contemporary discrimination and racism, we need to connect what we feel with what we think, the choices we make with how we behave. Developing emotional literacy, therefore, is the first focal point of the framework called Deep Diversity.

He Who Hesitates

Pleased with having selected a new pair of eyeglasses from a trusted shop, a consultant realizes he needs an updated prescription. The owner of the eyewear store recommends a local optometrist who does eye tests. She hands over a business card.

The consultant goes home and looks at the plain, unimpressive business card. He reads the name: Abdeiso Kiyanfar. And then he hesitates, suddenly uncertain about the recommendation. An image arises of an older, unskilled "foreign" man in a musty, disorganized office. The consultant sets the card down, and the better part of a day passes before he recognizes how unfairly he's behaving towards the optometrist. This was a referral, after all. He pushes aside his hesitation and phones to make an appointment.

This story about a hesitation—an unstated manifestation of prejudice—is based on a true event, and it has some interesting plot twists.

First of all, the consultant in the story is a seasoned veteran in diversity and anti-racism issues. Second, his ethnicity is South Asian—he's a brown guy. The third interesting fact is that he is me.

I share this story to illustrate how vulnerable we all are—vulnerable to prejudice, racism, and bias. Also because it holds some deep lessons about discrimination and inclusion. I am certain that if the "plain, unimpressive" business card had said Adam Wright or Ellen Goldstein, I would not have hesitated. And I would not have needed a referral, either, to take a chance on an unknown quantity with the "right" name. It's my hesitation—a brief moment of inaction—that's the issue.

Imagine if I were a hiring manager reviewing resumés and hesitated in the same way because a non-white name like Abdeiso Kiyanfar evoked a negative response? Or if I was a landlord renting an apartment and was turned off by "foreign-sounding" names? We all threaten fairness when such unconscious reluctance or preferences guide our decision-making processes in relating to others.

Project Implicit, a collaboration between Harvard University, University of Virginia, and the University of Washington, would describe this hesitation—this first negative association with a "foreign-sounding" name—as my *implicit* or unconscious bias.[7] (An interesting thing, given that my name, Shakil Choudhury, would also be considered outside the norm by most North American standards.)

This is the second important insight regarding issues of diversity and inclusion. *As humans, we all have biases we are not aware of that play out on a daily basis.*

According to Mahzarin Banaji, one of the great minds behind Project Implicit, our implicit biases exist not on a conscious thinking level, but entirely on the unconscious, emotional plane.[8] Implicit bias may be invisible to us, but it is more obvious to those who are impacted by it. Multiple studies demonstrate that such unconscious prejudice accurately predicts our behaviours.[9] Consequently, understanding and uncovering implicit bias is the second part of the Deep Diversity lens.

Not till You Drink Like Us

In a suburban setting, a man sits quietly watching a video. The images on the screen are of a mundane, repetitive nature: a man drinking a glass of water. The only variation is that the person shown drinking the water occasionally changes, from a white man to a black man, to an East Asian or South Asian one.

During this unremarkable experience, something unusual starts to happen. Unbeknownst to the watcher, his brain responds differently to each image that he observes. An electroencephalograph (EEG machine) monitoring his brain activity indicates to the researchers in the University of Toronto Scarborough lab that he has greater empathy for those who share his racial background.[10]

When he watches a person of his own race, the motor-cortex area of his brain lights up as it would if he were doing the task himself. But when the person on the screen is of a different race, there is hardly a blip in the register. In fact, when some participants observed someone of a different race having a drink of water, their brains registered "as little activity as when they watched a blank screen."[11]

Thus, the third insight on diversity and inclusion. *We have greater empathy—more care and concern—for those who are most like ourselves.* Our relationship to those most like ourselves, our "tribes," is the third pillar of Deep Diversity. We'll explore how belonging to groups is not only a key driver of human behaviour but also helps form our sense of self—who we are. Furthermore, favouritism towards the dominant racial/ethnic tribe results in discrimination that becomes systemic in nature.

Beyond the Third Dimension: Power

Emotions. Bias. Tribes. Any element of this trio offers a formidable challenge to nurturing diversity and inclusion in society. But it gets even more complicated. The unconscious influence of these three psychological dimensions fuses with the legacies of history, politics, colonization, and economics, creating—and perpetuating—imbalanced power structures in society. The result is the entrenchment of historically high-status (more power) and low-status (less power) groups based on social identities such as race, gender, class, sexual orientation, ability, and religion.

Group status and power can sometimes be obscured in societies like those of Canada or the United States. Here, fairness and equality are highly valued, and overt forms of discrimination, especially on the basis of race, are no longer acceptable in mainstream society. Yet subtle, less visible forms of bias are still pervasive across institutions. They are intimately linked to the way that power in society is divided along racial lines.

For example, few white people are likely to know that their names give them an invisible advantage in the job market. But in fact, those with white-sounding names are 40 to 50 per cent more likely to receive a callback for a job interview than applicants with black- or Asian-sounding names. A light skin colour also increases one's chances of receiving better health care and decreases the likelihood of being a victim of police shootings. Studies that we'll look at in upcoming chapters demonstrate that this type of discrimination is prevalent and systemic. Invisible benefits or drawbacks come with belonging or not belonging to the racial norm in society.

This is the final insight offered by the Deep Diversity framework. *Even in egalitarian, democratic societies, power needs to be named, challenged, and equalized to create greater fairness between racial groups.*

Unlike old-fashioned symbols of bigotry such as burning crosses, this form of racism is subtle and difficult for most of us to discuss. There's a simple reason: it is hidden. It requires talking about data—the collection and analysis of the experiences of thousands of people. Such data is abstract and inherently depersonalizes the conversation for some people, while activating—at times enraging—others because it verifies their experience. And this hidden racism, when named, can further polarize the rift between groups as it identifies which racial groups have more social power and less.

The problem is exemplified by the public conversations about racial profiling following the 2012 shooting death of an unarmed black teen, Trayvon Martin. He was killed by a gun-toting twenty-eight-year-old man in Sanford, Florida.[12]

A local newspaper editor, who is white, is quoted as saying: "Until this latest incident, race didn't seem to be a huge issue in Sanford. . . . Even now, after it's happened, I still think Sanford is a non-racist town."

The head of a Sanford diversity organization, a man of colour, responded by saying, "I understand white folks saying that . . . but there are blacks in this community who have lived through [racism] a long time."

In 2014, a similar thing happened after the death of another young black male, Michael Brown, who was shot by a white police officer in Ferguson, Missouri. Weeks of protests by black people (and their allies) followed, clearly articulating the alienation and persecution they experience. The white mayor of Ferguson, in contrast, said he was unaware of any racial frustrations before that tragic shooting that made them the centre of global headlines.[13]

Fifty years after the civil rights movement, the essence of the problem we struggle with in Canada and the United States is still captured by these two statements. *Race isn't an issue*, says the white person. *Racism is a problem that's always been here*, insists the person of colour.

Us. Them. On one side are millions who say they are experiencing a major difficulty that not only limits their ability to go after their dreams and get ahead but also threatens their physical lives. On the other side, millions of people say they don't see the problem and question whether it's actually "that bad." Frequently, they suggest that there may be other explanations.

Of course, no group sees any issue uniformly. Racialized people disagree with one another; whites disagree with whites. Yet public polls still demonstrate a significant racial divide over time on the topics of discrimination and prejudice in society.[14] (See sidebar: Polls Show Racial Divide.)

In cases like Trayvon Martin's and Michael Brown's, as the rhetoric and pain increases on both sides, so do the extreme positions. Hurtful words are spoken: *Racist! I hate white people. White justice doesn't serve us. Race-baiter! Blacks are criminals and deserve to be racially profiled . . .*

The cycle of Us versus Them repeats itself again and again. It usually comes out around an episode of violence against or death of a person of colour at the hands of a white person with power, like a police officer. A sample of names on this tragic list includes J.J. Harper in Winnipeg (1988), Rodney King in Los Angeles (1991), Faraz Suleman in Toronto (1996), Amadou Diallo in New York (1999), Fredy Villanueva in Montreal (2008), and Eric Garner in Staten Island (2014).

These are just a handful of cases from an enormous pile of evidence that racial profiling exists, in the criminal justice system generally and in policing specifically. In Canada alone, over fifteen reports since the 1970s have shown this.[15] It's a topic that's been studied to death for more than forty

POLLS SHOW RACIAL DIVIDE

Pew Research results after the Michael Brown shooting showed that 80 per cent of blacks felt the shooting "raised issues that need to be discussed"; only 37 per cent of white people felt the same way (Drake). The same poll revealed that 76 per cent of blacks had little or no confidence in ensuing police investigations, whereas 52 per cent of whites did.

Following the Trayvon Martin case, 68 per cent of racialized people felt the criminal justice system was biased against them, while only 32 per cent of whites agreed that there was a pro-white bias (Newport). The racial divide was persistent in spite of the complication that the man who shot Martin was a biracial man, son of a white father and a Peruvian mother (Fish).

Sources:

Bruce Drake, "Ferguson Highlights Deep Divisions between Blacks and Whites in America," Pew Research Center, www.pewresearch.org, Nov. 26, 2014.

Jefferson M. Fish, "What Race Is George Zimmerman?" *Psychology Today: Looking in the Cultural Mirror,* www.psychologytoday.com, Aug. 13, 2013.

Frank Newport, "Blacks, Nonblacks Hold Sharply Different Views of Martin Case: Blacks More Likely to Believe Race Is a Major Factor," *Gallup,* www.gallup.com, April 5, 2012.

years. Yet, as a public conversation, it's a train wreck. We talk about it like we're unruly beginners.

And it's not entirely our fault.

I've come to believe that to understand what's going on, we must go deeper than skin colour, both literally and figuratively. Our core struggles regarding Us versus Them lie hidden in the architecture of our brains. The way that we are neurologically wired is compounded through the processes of being socialized and by the power dynamics between racial groups.

Emotionally charged issues like racial profiling so easily trigger an Us/Them dynamic because much of what's happening is below the radar of awareness, hidden even from ourselves. Our state of "autopilot," that is, our default position—what we can't see—has great influence. And it's often unhelpful. As a result, situations, issues, and choices repeat themselves over and over.

A Compassionate Approach
for Tackling Contemporary Racism

Once you know why change is so hard, you can drop the brute force method and take a more psychologically sophisticated approach.
– Jonathan Haidt, social psychologist, NYU Stern School of Business[16]

For twenty years now, I've been an educator and consultant on issues of diversity and inclusion. I help organizations work through their differences, to nurture environments where all people feel like they matter and belong. Our team at Anima Leadership is called in to train staff and students when a school has a racist incident. We are consulted when a human rights settlement requires an intervention. Our team has also developed trainings, curricula, and measurement tools for federal and provincial governments in Canada and assisted private and public sector organizations to improve their diversity outcomes. Internationally, I've led intercultural dialogue projects for communities in conflict, specifically in Europe and South America.

For a long time, I believed that issues of racism and discrimination were simply a matter of ignorance. I thought that if we, as good citizens in egalitarian, democratic societies had the "right" information, we would make better, more thoughtful and fair choices. Gradually I discovered that this appeal-to-the-head-and-behaviour-will-change strategy—a cognitive approach to social change—works only in a limited manner.

As the opening vignettes indicate, the problem is much more complex than being misinformed. The Yale-York-British Columbia study demonstrated that even young, educated, and ethnoculturally diverse students have a significant discrepancy between what they think and feel about discrimination, and what they actually *do* in the face of a racist event. The drinking water study from University of Toronto suggests that we have greater empathy for those who are racially most like ourselves. And my own story about hesitating at the optometrist's name shows the presence of unconscious bias even in someone whose life work is to educate others about issues of discrimination and difference.

An irrational preference for a white over a black student. Greater empathy for those of our own race. A hesitation.

Notice the subtlety of each of these three examples. There are no neo-Nazis, no segregation, and no deliberate persecution. In short, there are no signs of our ugly and easily identified villain, overt racism. Yet all three examples are manifestations of its slyer yet still toxic twin, subtle racism— also referred to as *systemic discrimination.* This form of racism is hard to see and therefore even harder to discuss. As exemplified by the public conversations about racial profiling following the tragic deaths of Trayvon Martin and Michael Brown, it can easily fracture groups along racial lines.

And this is what's holding us back collectively. This book will argue that overcoming systemic discrimination is the next part of the incomplete historical social project towards racial justice. The Deep Diversity framework can offer a non-judgmental, comprehensive approach to nurturing inclusion in both organizations and communities.

In short, Deep Diversity exposes some hard-to-see intergroup dynamics. It makes both our brain (cognition) and heart (emotions) vulnerable to constructive change. It's learning to ask four key questions when faced with issues of ethnocultural and racial differences:

- What are the influences of emotions?
- What are the influences of bias?
- What are the influences of tribes?
- What are the influences of power?

Using Brain Science to Understand Us/Them

At the heart of the Us versus Them dynamic is our tendency to see a person as a symbol of a group, especially of a racial or ethnic group, rather than as an individual.[17] When we do this, our empathy is reduced and we may dehumanize the person in some small or big way. Research described as "robust" demonstrates our tendency to see those who are racially different in simplistic, primitive stereotypes—more like animals or objects than people.[18] This tendency, called *infrahumanization* or objectification, shows itself whenever we make generalizations about a sub-set of people, especially so-called minority groups. (For example, associating blacks with apes and violence, or seeing East Asians as hard-working, expressionless, almost robotically efficient.)

Fundamental to this discussion is understanding that our unconscious mind—automatic, reactive, emotional, and intuitive—easily dominates the conscious mind, the realm of logic, language, reason, and abstraction.[19] (See sidebar: Brain-Mind Phenomenon.) In the words of a respected researcher, Joseph Ledoux of New York University, "Consciousness may get all the focus . . . but consciousness is a small part of what the brain does, and it's a slave to everything that works beneath it."[20]

As this book will show, our unconscious biases and automatic brain processes frequently favour those most "like us," creating racial blind spots and hard-to-see discrimination that become systemic against "them." This causes many hard-working individuals and groups to be hurt or prevented from moving forward in society because of their ethnocultural or racial background. We'll also explore how power dynamics and group status make things more complicated. Many minority group members also dehumanize themselves, while favouring the dominant racial group's members, characteristics, and values.

Turning inwards to the level of gut feelings and emotions will offer a greater appreciation of the problem, as well as possible solutions. As we appreciate the depth of what we collectively face and are able to generate some compassion for why we get stuck, we may be better positioned to progress towards racial equality in new, more helpful directions.

In brain science terms, we have to disrupt and alter the neural pathways that result in biases that do not serve us collectively.[21] In plain language, we have to break some bad habits regarding issues of racial difference.

BRAIN-MIND PHENOMENON

The words *brain* and *mind* are related but not interchangeable terms. The brain is the physical organ encased by our skull. "The mind is what the brain does," according to neuropsychologist Rick Hanson.

Modern cognitive science describes the mind as having two tracks. Track 1, known as the adaptive unconscious, functions behind the scenes as a giant biological computer. It is fast, automatic, effortless, reactive, and emotionally charged.

What most people are most familiar with, however, is Track 2, the conscious mind, which is explicit, deliberate, and sequential and requires effort to use. Ideas, thoughts, rationality, and language—so highly valued in society—are the domain of the conscious mind.

It is a great surprise to many people to learn that that the thinking mind is dominated by the unconscious mind. Contrary to popular belief, we do not think our way through life. We *feel* our way.

Sources:

Rick Hanson, *Buddha's Brain: The Practical Neuroscience of Happiness, Love and Wisdom* (Oakland, CA: New Harbinger Publications Inc., 2009), 34–36.

David G. Myers, "The Powers and Perils of Intuition: Understanding the Nature of Our Gut Instincts," *Scientific American Mind* (June–July 2007): 24.

Breaking Bad Habits; Nurturing Good Ones

To say that we, as humans, are creatures of habit is a profound understatement. By *habit* I'm referring to something much bigger than a daily ritual of grabbing a coffee before work or going to the gym at set times. Most of our waking life is habit-based, from our posture, walking gait, sense of confidence, manner of speaking, accent, and favourite expressions to how we think, chew, eat, feel, laugh, move, play, or sleep.

A significant part of our lives, therefore, is experienced in a state of autopilot. We don't think about what we do, we just do it.[22] This is both the brilliance and drawback of our neural architecture. For example, learned behaviour that becomes unconscious (such as driving a car) allows us to function efficiently. It frees up our mind to pay attention to new, less familiar things in our environment (a driver in the wrong lane) and prioritize our actions (swerve out of the way).

If we had to pay conscious attention to all the stimuli in our environment at any given moment (all the minor and major tasks required in driving a car), even basic events would be overwhelming. We couldn't focus on what was important, which could put us in harm's way. The flip side is that such autopilot results in filters and bias, and a state of comfort with how things are. This makes change difficult for us.

Habits are also larger than the individual. Habits shared by a large group of people—whether in a corporation, profession, or nation—become *social norms* (also called *cultural norms*). Our environment marinates us in these customs, behaviours, and thinking patterns. They range from what side of the road we drive on to how we greet people (handshakes or kisses), how much eye contact we make (sign of respect or disrespect), and what kinds of clothing or public displays of affection are acceptable. We are social beings whose individual identities are influenced by a wide variety of forces, including ethnic and gender norms, family, friends, co-workers, communities, social class, and religion, to name just a few.

A large body of research demonstrates that many social norms are invisible (for example, greeting a stranger with a handshake) until they are breached (being greeted with kisses on both cheeks by someone you don't know).[23] And the experience of norms being broken can often be emotional. We might have a sense that something is not right or feel confusion, embarrassment, or anger. As a result, we may begin to avoid specific people, places, or situations.

Whether such habits are learned or genetically influenced, they are usually unconscious. Our culture, then, provides the "software" that both helps and hinders racial interactions. But the Deep Diversity framework also explores the "hardware" side of things. It turns out that we are biologically predisposed to bias and discrimination. We are preprogrammed from birth to seek out our tribe and define who is part of it and who is not.

This aspect of the research demonstrates that bias, fear, and prejudice are intertwined in the mind with normal processes of how we perceive, categorize, remember, and learn.[24] It seems to suggest that the mechanisms for Us versus Them are, at least partially, built into the human design. From my experience, accepting and admitting this is a good collective starting point. It gives us permission to have conversations about bias, prejudice, and discrimination that otherwise are almost taboo. After all, how can we talk productively about prejudice and discrimination if these concepts are associated only with neo-Nazis and overt racists but not with the rest of us?

Enhancing diversity, inclusion, and equity requires both learning and unlearning about others and ourselves. It requires developing more psychologically sophisticated strategies to advance diversity and inclusion. In short, it requires us to break generations of bad racial habits and nurture good ones. Unless we understand the roles played by both hardware and software components in our mental processes, fairness and justice will always be threatened in our personal, professional, and community lives.

The Deep Diversity Model

The Deep Diversity approach described in this book argues that we must understand the brain and mind—its conscious and unconscious dimensions. The psychobiology underlying human behaviour motivates racial interactions as well as socialization processes. On one level, Deep Diversity is simply a framework that asks, when faced with issues of racial and ethnic differences: What are the influences of emotions, of bias, of tribes, and of power?

On another level, it's about disrupting and debugging the Us/Them default setting that the human program is predisposed to. Attempting to answer the four Deep Diversity questions makes possible a more nuanced understanding of what's happening for us and to us.

Each of the four key questions can be a gateway into a series of related questions. For example, the question of *emotions* in a racial situation, which chapter 2 focuses on, may generate the following:

- What do I feel about this situation, group, or issue?
- What do others who are involved in this situation, group, or issue feel?
- What is the emotional tone or characteristic of this situation, group, or issue?
- What is the emotional history behind this situation, group, or issue? How might that history still influence perspectives and outcomes today?
- How do we address the needs underlying what people are feeling?

Similar questions need to be generated on the topics of bias, tribes, and power. Chapter 3 demonstrates that all humans have implicit *biases* that result in personal, collective, and societal blind spots regarding issues of racial difference. Such invisible prejudices lead to behaviours that can undermine fairness and impair judgment, with outcomes that can be mild (for example, social slights) to severe (violence and death).

Chapter 4 explores the concept of *tribes*. Belonging to groups is a significant driver of human behaviour, as important as the need for food, water, and shelter. Our sense of who we are as individuals is developed through our interactions in groups both consciously and unconsciously. Such tribes form and divide along socially important lines such as race, ethnicity, religion, or gender. They also develop for more arbitrary reasons, such as team colours or who sits where in an office.

Chapter 5 focuses on *power*, exploring the interplay of social power between dominant and non-dominant groups. This is a critical lens in tackling systemic forms of discrimination such as racism. Power is a complicated subject, though, that requires more than a single chapter. Exploring this topic is double-edged, and can feel both empowering and overwhelming. Chapter 6, therefore, is unconventional and explores *personal power*. This section argues that developing resilience by beefing up our psychological and spiritual qualities is important to advancing diversity and inclusion, as well as preventing burnout. The conclusion of the book, in chapter 7, brings all the pieces of the Deep Diversity framework together.

Neuroplasticity: Changing Habits of the Mind

Deep Diversity focuses on habit breaking and forming. It is entirely possible to change our habits: there are proven ways to change how we think and perceive, thereby developing new neural patterns. There is considerable evidence of *neuroplasticity*, meaning that where we put our attention and what we focus on helps change the structures of the brain.[25] Just as muscle mass can increase through physical workouts, we can grow parts of our brain, allowing us to form new habits and shift our perspectives in the ongoing task of increasing racial harmony.

Many of the strategies outlined in this book build on the principle that thinking influences actions, similar to cognitive-behavioural therapy (see sidebar). CBT is an evidence-based form of treatment that has been used since the 1960s to help people change unproductive ways of thinking and behaving.[26] It has proven successful in helping people address a wide variety of issues, including depression, anxiety, eating disorders, anger management, post-traumatic stress disorder, and low self-esteem.[27] Why not consider similar principles to tackle prejudice and stereotypes? After all, biases and preconceptions about others are, in many ways, just distortions in our thinking. Change the thinking, change the behaviour.

Inner Skills and Compassion Support Deep Diversity

In the words of neuropsychologist Rick Hanson, "you can do small things inside your mind that will lead to big changes in your brain and your experience of living."[28] Deep Diversity emphasizes that we can change how we think and feel about others and ourselves, especially regarding racial issues, so as not to be unconsciously swept away by ancient brain processes and structures. It requires some work and effort, but it is entirely possible.

These "small things" that Dr. Hanson refers to I'll call *inner skills*, as they have to do with what's going on inside our individual heads and bod-

COGNITIVE-BEHAVIOURAL THERAPY TO TACKLE BIAS

Cognitive-behavioural therapy was developed in the 1960s by psychiatrist Aaron Beck to tackle depression. In short, it involves a few simple steps:

- Observe our thoughts that are unhelpful (for example, *I'm bad at interviews*) as they influence our feelings (increased anxiety) and actions (cancel the interview).
- Rather than simply reacting, evaluate the distortion or inaccuracy in the thought. (*I'm aware of my fear and strong urge to cancel the interview. But this is just a bad habit.*)
- Create alternate options of thinking and acting. (*I'm very capable and I'm going to go for it, regardless.*)

Similar principles are built upon in Deep Diversity to tackle subtle prejudice and discrimination.

ies. These are micro-abilities that help us stay centred and balanced when things get emotionally heated. We can call on them when controversy clouds our thinking and threatens to divide people along lines of race, ethnicity, and identity.

Each chapter will introduce one or two inner skills to enhance positive relationships with ourselves and others. The skills—self-awareness, meditation, self-regulation, empathy, self-education, relationship management, conflict skills, and meaning making—serve as the action component to the Deep Diversity model. These skills can be developed and enhanced. And they can help us nurture greater ease, resiliency, and flexibility in dealing with others.

Compassion, the "mental state of wishing that others may be free from suffering," is the underlying principle for all of this work.[29] It is needed because diversity, by its very nature, is about our differences. It is about the places where we are not, and may never be, the same. We will—we must—make mistakes, both big and small. That's part of the process of learning about each other. But making mistakes feels bad, so most of us have learned to avoid, deny, or minimize them.

When walking through the field of diversity, pebbled with mistake-making opportunities, our "secret power" is compassion. Turned inwards, self-compassion can help soothe the voice of the inner critic that judges harshly and tends to dwell on errors and missteps, preventing us from moving forward. It can help us all accept that humans—regardless of background, colour, or identity—are imperfect creatures. We are all on a learning curve regarding unconscious prejudice and intergroup dynamics. Accepting this as part of the process may help us move past the internal and external judgments that hinder learning.

As we begin to grasp the impersonal nature of prejudice and discrimination—that it's a leftover of primitive elements of our brain—we can generate more compassion for others and ourselves. Some of our struggles are a result of neural hardwiring, shaping a good amount of our "group-ish" nature. However, a significant amount—a result of socialization, norms, and socio-economic structures—is changeable. The former is not our fault, but the latter is our responsibility.

Intentional Focus on Race

Although Deep Diversity has implications for a variety of equity issues—including gender, class, sexual orientation, and ability—this book will specifically focus on race and ethnicity. This focus is intentionally narrow. It will allow us to drill down into one specific area and apply the framework comprehensively. As we understand the patterns of difference more clearly and grasp the hair-trigger tendency to fracture into "us" and "them," the possibility emerges of creating a map for other equity issues.

This book is steeped in my identity as a middle-class, heterosexual, able-bodied, university-educated Canadian male of South Asian ethnicity. I was born in Pakistan, the child of two parents originally from pre-partition India with family today on both sides of that border, representing Islam as well as Hinduism. We went through the immigrant shuffle of 1970s Canada before my family landed on its feet in the 1980s. I claim my identity and personal journey as the source of strength and insight for this book, and openly name it as the basis of bias and weakness, both conscious and unconscious. I don't believe we can ever be truly objective; our worldview is always tainted through our personal filters. But we can be transparent about our starting points.

I'm also not a psychologist or neuroscientist. I have, therefore, provided citations for the research to back up my claims, and stayed within ideas that are generally accepted in these fields. I've also invited a wide variety of professionals, including those with science and psychology expertise, to review my writing. The final decisions, however, are mine alone, and I take full responsibility for what's written here. Just as professional coaches in the business world know they are not therapists and can only work to a certain level of depth with clients, I have learned to be respectful of my professional boundaries. But I've also had to step beyond my field of expertise, developing an interdisciplinary approach that I think is important to share.

That's my entry point.

Regardless of your starting point in this conversation about diversity and fairness, the journey ahead is a shared one. It's about all of us as humans—there is no "them." The collective step, however, begins with the individual. It begins with each of us venturing out of our comfort zones and taking a risk, trying something new.

In the words of world-famous musician Yo-Yo Ma: "Things can fall apart, or threaten to, for many reasons, and then there's got to be a leap of faith. Ultimately, when you're at the edge, you have to go forward or backward; if you go forward, you have to jump together."[30]

2

EMOTIONS:
UNDERSTANDING
OURSELVES AND OTHERS

Crisp Winters, Burning Women

THE PHOTOS on the website are inviting. This kind of small-town pastoral splendour is like catnip for city dwellers like me: flowing rivers, lush forests, kids and horses, and even a beautiful white church with tall spires. The site goes on to say that "the surrounding countryside is reminiscent of times past, lazy country summer days, crystal clear streams and lakes with cold crisp winters in an unspoiled environment."[1]

Wow—I'm in. Sign me up.

Clicking through the site, I find something called the town charter, which has been approved by the mayor and six council members. The declaration includes a section entitled "Our Women."

Hmmm . . . interesting. I scroll down and read:

We consider that men and women are of the same value. Having said this, we consider that a woman can; drive a car, vote, sign checks, dance, decide for herself, speak her peace [*sic*], dress as she sees fit respecting of course the democratic decency, walk alone in public places, study, have a job, have her own belongings and anything else that a man can do. These are our standards and our way of life.

This is starting to sound somewhat unusual. What is it—perhaps the website of a commune or a retreat centre with pseudo-feminist leanings? The last line, though, really throws a wrench in the works:

> However, we consider that killing women in public, beatings, or burning them alive are not part of our standards of life.

Wow. What part of the world could promise both cold crisp winters and a strong rebuke against burning women, advertised in the community's code of conduct? Confused yet?

Welcome to Herouxville, Canada. Population: 1,200 people.

In 2007, this community in the French-speaking province of Quebec made national and international headlines when it passed the now infamous Herouxville Town Charter. (The original charter even forbade the "stoning of women.") The context? No local or regional cases of such gender-based violence prompted the town's charter. It seemed a not-so-subtle message targeting "immigrant" groups, specifically Muslims. But immigrants (and people of colour, generally) are almost non-existent in this very white region of the country. So where was this coming from?

There were no actual experiences or problems in the region, let alone the village, upon which to base this aspect of the town charter. We are left to speculate why the town council would take such drastic steps. I'll leave that question hanging for a moment, as the actions of this small town were a harbinger of things to come on a larger scale.

Six years later, the provincial government of that same province—the recently elected Parti Québécois, a party whose existence is premised on Quebec separating from Canada and forming its own independent country—drew a page from the Herouxville playbook. It proposed a so-called Charter of Quebec Values that promoted an extreme form of secularism in the name of "neutrality." The centrepiece was to ban the wearing of all overt religious symbols—including Muslim hijabs, Sikh turbans, Jewish kippahs, and large Christian crosses—by public employees including doctors, teachers, government officials, and daycare workers.

Further, it was proposed that publicly funded daycare centres would be forbidden from serving halal or kosher foods, sidelining students from families that practised these religious observations. People would be allowed to wear small, "discreet" items like rings or pendants, although what was defined as discreet was unclear. The only exception would be a number of Catholic symbols, including street names and large crosses or crucifixes that would continue to hang in public places, as a way of acknowledging Quebec's religious-cultural history.

Incidents of minorities being harassed increased dramatically. Observant Muslims, in particular, reported property damage, confrontations, and being spat on publicly.[2] Canadians, including many Quebecers, were outraged and polarized by these events.

In the cases of both Herouxville and the proposed Quebec secular charter, mainstream analyses focused on anti-immigrant prejudice, Islamophobia, and the urban-rural divide. Some political observers suggested that the Parti Québécois's use of such divisive political tactics was a gamble on the part of a desperate party whose separatist mandate had an aging and shrinking support base. Mobilizing conservative, rural voters—the PQ's foundation—was strategic, as these people had the strongest ties to the traditional French-speaking, Euro-cultural heritage of the province.

But what I find most relevant to the Deep Diversity discussion is that in this conversation, fear was a critical undercurrent. Why is fear so easily triggered? When it comes to dealing with those whom we perceive to be cultural outsiders, why is it so easy to evoke feelings of anxiety, suspicion, or even panic? The emotion of fear—often present in these situations but usually invisible—opens a way to examine the broader unseen role emotions play in our encounters with those who are, or are perceived to be, different than us.

Investigating fear as a trigger allows us to expose and thereby weaken the unconscious power of Us versus Them. This dynamic can manipulate us into being reactive rather than thoughtful, resulting in choices that sometimes hurt our relationships and communities. We'll also discuss how the inner skill of self-awareness can help us identify what's happening internally, so that when it comes to issues of racial difference, we are better able to act rather than react.

I'll focus on the Herouxville Town Charter to make this point. But similar dynamics play out at all levels of government (and institutions), often obscured by multiple layers of politics.

Developing Emotional Literacy

Emotions do more than colour our sensory world; they are at the root of everything we do, the unquenchable origin of every act more complicated than a reflex.

– Lewis, Amini, and Lannon, *A General Theory of Love*[3]

In the 1990s, psychologist Daniel Goleman helped popularize the principles of emotional intelligence. Since then, a considerable library of materials has developed on the purpose and power of emotions and their controlling yet invisible role in our lives. Developing our emotional quotient (EQ) has become widely recognized as critical to personal and organizational success. EQ is regarded by many to be as important as IQ (intelligence quotient), the traditional measure of intelligence.[4]

In daily life, emotional intelligence can be defined simply as how well we, as individuals, manage ourselves in relationships with others. This sounds deceptively simple. Most of us believe that we handle ourselves pretty well and would likely say that we are good at managing our relationships. Where a relationship is not easy, even while accepting some responsibility, we're likely to point to shortcomings in the other person. *They* are angry, self-centred, and insecure. It's rare that we notice how our own actions, tone, or behaviour may have contributed to or instigated the problem.

Even when we pay lip service to the idea that we're not perfect, we put our energy into finding fault in the other. Through this exercise of fault-finding, it's difficult to see other people clearly. Our unconscious motivations, bias, fear, and history—our emotional baggage—gets in the way.

This is especially true regarding issues of diversity and intergroup differences. Emotions play a crucial role in the Us/Them dynamic. Feelings are at the roots of our actions, whether we are aware of them or not. A significant portion of our decision making lies below the surface of our awareness. That's why developing emotional literacy is critical.

From a mountain of good literature on this topic, here are three ideas that are helpful for understanding the unconscious and automatic nature of emotions as they are relevant to issues of racial difference:

- *Tilting towards/away:* We are inclined to tilt towards or away from things in our environment; this is also called the *approach-withdrawal system*. Whether we are aware of it or not, we tend to tilt towards those most like ourselves and away from those we perceive to be different.
- *Emotional contagion:* The contagious nature of emotions and the open-loop structure of our nervous systems means we are designed to regulate each other. When we feel included, we tend to soar. When excluded, we tend to underperform, second-guess ourselves, and in extreme cases, get sick.
- *Emotional triggers:* The midbrain region, called the limbic system, modulates our emotions; the amygdala specifically alerts us to dangers in our environment. Strong emotional triggers can activate the *fight-flight-freeze* response, reducing our ability to think clearly, especially when dealing with those who are racially different than us.

Tilting Towards/Away: Our Survival Instincts

The primitive nature of our brain is well established in research: it was designed to survive physical threats and emergencies more than anything else.[5] (See sidebar: Primitive Brain Served Our Ancestors Well.) Although that function may have suited our ancient cave-dwelling relatives who lived

PRIMITIVE BRAIN SERVED OUR ANCESTORS WELL

From an evolutionary perspective, the brain was designed to survive physical threats and emergencies. It is believed that our brain's primal orientation towards a *fight-flight-freeze* response helped our cave-dwelling ancestors—who lived in tribes of thirty to seventy people with a fraction of our life expectancy—survive through extremely violent times.

Threats in their natural environment included dangerous animals and plants as well as other humans. Daily survival frequently depended on reacting swiftly, without time for careful thinking. Researchers suggest that early humans, similarly to our animal cousins, survived thanks to the reactive, unconscious, adaptive nature of the brain.

Although our prefrontal cortex—the thinking brain—has expanded significantly over the millions of years of evolution, the basic brain orientation towards emergencies can still override rationality and reason. This reactive, defensive part of our neural wiring serves us less well in an interconnected village of seven billion people.

Sources:

Daniel Goleman, Richard E. Boyatsis, and Annie Mckee, *Primal Leadership: Learning to Lead with Emotional Intelligence* (Boston: Harvard Business Press, 2002, 2004).

Thomas Lewis, Fari Amini, and Richard Lannon, *A General Theory of Love* (New York: Vintage Books, 2000).

Daniel J. Siegel, *Mindsight: The New Science of Personal Transformation* (New York: Bantam Books Trade Paperbacks, 2011).

in small, violent tribes, it can be problematic for interconnected, globalized societies in which billions of people are attempting to live together.

Like other animals, we have a very simple survival orientation: tilting either towards or away from things. Generally, we are attracted to tasty foods, pleasant smells, friendly people, warm blankets when we feel cool, and cold drinks when we're hot. At the same time, we will jump away if we think we see a snake, express disgust at rotting foods and animals, pull our hands back from a hot fire, and generally avoid erratic or dangerous people.

Overall, both tilts are part of an elaborate mechanism to help us keep our physical and emotional states in balance.[6] The approach-withdrawal system develops from genetics as well as social and environmental factors. It also applies to our relation to human groups based on identity: we gravitate to those who are most like ourselves, and are shy or fearful of those who are different.

Negative Tilt Stronger Than Positive

It's important to note, however, that the two tilts are not created equal: the tendency to withdraw is more powerful than the tendency to approach. We have what's known as a *negativity bias* that primes us for avoidance and remembering the bad even when it's outnumbered by the good.[7]

From my experience working with people—whether with junior high school students or with senior management teams—people will spend much more time discussing, for example, what went wrong at the end of a project rather than what went right. It's rarely proportional. The negatives are almost always given far more airtime than is deserved. The positives are skimmed over relatively quickly.

Rick Hanson describes this phenomenon as the brain's tendency to be "like Velcro for negative experiences and Teflon for positive ones."[8] Of course, people don't need to have advanced psychology degrees to figure this out. It's why political smear campaigns are so effective and why news reports seek to attract an audience by focusing on what's going wrong in the world.

Well established in research, this negativity bias is much less overt than a conscious thought. It exists instead at the subtle feeling level. It's also closely related to fear, which is believed to be our oldest emotion.[9] As a result, we recognize fearful faces more quickly than happy or neutral ones. One brain structure related to emotions, the amygdala, is activated so quickly when fearful faces are flashed that they don't even need to be registered consciously.[10] The impact has also been shown in relationship to diversity. Greater negativity arises when dealing with those we perceive to be different than ourselves, especially racially.[11]

We can track this tendency back to early humans. It would have been an evolutionary advantage to tune in to danger, fear, aggression, and general negativity expressed by unfamiliar people who may have been a threat to survival.

Much research, which this chapter and the next will expand upon, demonstrates that we generally tilt towards those most like ourselves while tilting away from those who are different. This impacts our choices of where we live, work, and play and whom we choose to be part of our social networks.

For example, just northwest of Toronto in the suburb of Brampton, where my family lived for many years, a massive influx of South Asians took place over the last two decades. This group now makes up almost 40 per cent of the population. (In fact, people of colour are a majority there, with over 60 per cent of the population).[12] Many people whose roots are from India and Pakistan have made this place their home, drawn to a city that has a lot of people like them (tilt towards). This is far from unusual; such ethnic enclaves—Chinese, Italian, Greek, Polish, Jewish—have always existed, in some variation, in most large cities.

On the other hand, *white flight* describes the phenomenon in which white people have left Brampton—and other North American city cores— in significant numbers. Many felt uncomfortable with their place in the increasing ethnocultural diversity (tilt away), preferring more homogenous white communities and small towns outside the city (tilt towards).[13]

In the context of Herouxville, negativity bias may help us understand how the fear of difference became so easily activated, even when there was little local experience with immigrants or people of diverse backgrounds. The town charter seems to have emerged from a defensive posture, a wariness of imagined immigrants. In contrast, the mayor of another small town in Quebec—Huntington, population 2,587—made headlines in 2011 through a tilt towards newcomers. He announced his intention to build a mosque, halal slaughterhouse, and Muslim cemetery to entice highly educated immigrants to help counter his community's population decline.[14]

Emotional Contagion:
Being Controlled by the Moods of Others

The open-loop design of the limbic system means that other people can change our very physiology—and so our emotions.
– Goleman, Boyatzis, and McKee, *Primal Leadership*[15]

Emotions surround all human dynamics, influencing our interactions on conscious and unconscious levels. Many experiments demonstrate that feelings are contagious. They can be transferred between people, like catching a cold.[16] Our heart rate, blood pressure, and mood, for example, are easily synchronized with others in our vicinity. Those who are emotionally dominant can transfer their mood to others without effort, prior history, or words being spoken. (For more details, see sidebar: Emotions Are Invisible and Contagious.)

These effects, referred to generally as *emotional contagion*, occur with family and friends, in boardrooms, on the shop floor, or when dealing with clients and customers.[17] Emotions spread quickly and easily, influencing interactions in our private, public, and professional lives.

The physical form of our bodies can convince us that we are a series of self-contained units—closed loops—that are separate entities from other people. Although there is some truth to this (otherwise we would be leaking blood and fluids everywhere we went), it's also partly an illusion. Neurologically speaking, we are considered *open-loop systems*.[18]

Our nervous systems are designed to tune in to and intermingle with each other's physiology to make neural connections. Specifically, our emotions play a significant role in our biochemical regulation. We are designed to regulate, and be regulated by, others. (For more details, see sidebar: The Illusion of Separation.)

By design, we are also exquisitely sensitive to social pain such as exclusion and ostracism. In the words of neuroscientist Matthew D. Lieberman, "When human beings experience threats or damage to their social bonds, the brain responds in much the same way it responds to physical pain."[19]

EMOTIONS ARE INVISIBLE AND CONTAGIOUS

Emotions are a part of all human interactions, whether subtly or strongly, with or without our awareness. The influencing, at times contagious, nature of emotions is illustrated in the following examples:

- At the end of a fifteen-minute conversation between two research participants, their physiological profiles—including heart rate and blood pressure—look quite similar, even though their profiles were different from each other at the beginning of the conversation. This synchronization of physiology, called *emotional mirroring,* occurs in line with the strength of emotions being experienced: hardly at all during emotionally neutral conversations, subtly during pleasant ones, and most powerfully during conflicted, angry, and hurtful exchanges.
- Three strangers are seated in a room such that they are facing and can see each other, but do not talk during the experiment. Pretests determine the emotional state of each of the participants before they begin. Within minutes, all three participants share the same mood, each person in the group unconsciously synchronizing their emotional state with the others. The evidence also shows that the mood is transmitted by the most emotionally dominant/expressive person in the group. It should be stressed that this happens without them speaking or having any prior history with, or knowledge of, each other.
- Similar research examined the interactions of seventy teams across diverse industries ranging from health care to accounting. During meetings, all members of the group shared the same mood within two hours. The emotions of team members tracked together in synchronicity, independent of team hassles, successes, or failures.

Source:
Goleman, Boyatzis, and McKee, *Primal Leadership*, 5–9.

THE ILLUSION OF SEPARATION:
NEURAL WIRING CONNECTS US

When we experience the powerful sensation of being "in sync" with another person, it is an example of *emotional resonance.* This effect not only feels good, but is also a powerful tool that may be used by leaders and groups to drive collective emotions in a positive direction, creating enthusiasm and high performance. Professional teams that are on winning streaks and become seemingly unstoppable demonstrate the quality of emotional resonance.

We can also experience the opposite effect, that of *emotional dissonance.* This is the experience of feeling "out of step" with another person; the relationship seems awkward, clumsy, or always challenging. Leaders and groups with significant dissonance can create toxic environments where low morale, reduced productivity, and increased sick leave are common.

We are designed to regulate one another, on a deep, biochemical level. The conclusion that many researchers have reached is that emotions serve a critical role in human interactions that is necessary not just for our well-being, but for our very survival as a species (Lewis, Amini, and Lannon, 66–99).

Consider the following examples:

- Rene Spitz's famous research from the 1940s looked at babies in hygienic institutions whose basic needs were met (they were fed, clothed, cleaned, and kept warm) but who had limited physical human contact (were not held, stroked, or played with). These babies had staggeringly high death rates compared to those infants in the less pristine general public who were being held, fondled, and generally loved by caregivers (Lewis, Amini, and Lannon).
- A 2003 study measured the blood pressure of participants five minutes into every social interaction over a three-day period. Interactions with family members and spouses were found to lower blood pressure, while interactions with ambivalent network members were found to

produce the highest blood pressure (Holt-Lunstad, Uchino, and Smith).
- In 2012, the Amsterdam Study of the Elderly found that elderly people who lived alone were twice as likely (9.3 per cent) to develop dementia after three years compared to those who lived with others (5.6 per cent). Especially important was how people felt. Those who reported feeling lonely (13.4 per cent) developed dementia at twice the rate of those did not feel this way (5.7 per cent) (Holwerda et al.).

Sources:

Lewis, Amini, and Lannon, *A General Theory of Love*, 69–70.

Julianne Holt-Lunstad, Bert N. Uchino, and Timothy W. Smith, "Social Relationships and Ambulatory Blood Pressure: Structural and Qualitative Predictors of Cardiovascular Function during Everyday Social Interactions," *Health Psychology* 22,4 (2003), 388–97.

Tjalling Jan Holwerda et al., "Feelings of Loneliness, but not Social Isolation, Predict Dementia Onset: Results from the Amsterdam Study of the Elderly (AMSTEL)," *Journal of Neurology Neurosurgery and Psychiatry* 85,2 (2014), published online 2012, doi: 10.1136/jnnp-2012-302755.

Lieberman's team was the first to demonstrate that social and physical pain areas overlap in the same region of the brain.[20] Kipling D. Williams from Purdue University has shown that even brief experiences of exclusion during the playing of something as insignificant as an online game resulted in strong emotional reactions. Participants demonstrated "unusually low levels of belonging to groups or society, diminished self-esteem, and lack of meaning, and control over, their lives."[21]

The upside to this neural connection is that joy, positivity, calmness, and rationality can also be transferred between people. Emotional intelligence research has clearly shown that when individuals or groups feel positive and upbeat, everything goes better, including creativity, problem solving, productivity, understanding complexity, and predisposition to being helpful.[22]

The downside of our ability to regulate each other is that negative emotions like chronic anger, anxiety, or a sense of futility can also be transferred, damaging relationships and hijacking the work or personal environment. Generally, when we are upset, stress hormones are secreted that take many hours to be reabsorbed by the body and fade. They impact our ability to rest, sleep, and recover.[23] In a toxic workplace, for example, where conflict, distrust, or dysfunctional relations are the norm, not only is productivity reduced but the health impacts on employees can also be significant, resulting in sick leaves and absenteeism. In Canada, it is estimated that stress-related absences cost employers $3.5 billion annually, while in the United States, that figure is ballparked at $300 billion.[24]

Leaders Set the Emotional Tone

According to emotional intelligence research, leaders play a role in how people feel. In a group, they serve as emotional guides.[25] Leaders' words and reactions carry more weight than those of other group members; they are watched more carefully and are given more eye contact. We take many of our cues from those in charge.

People in positions of authority generally set the tone for appropriate group behaviour, especially in times of uncertainty. For example, leaders who are able to stay calm during a crisis can settle group members. A manager who demonstrates mild anxiety or hesitancy may communicate to the team that something still needs careful thought or attention. Leaders can inspire us, evoke our empathy, or fuel our patriotism and anger through a call to arms against an enemy. The quality of leadership, therefore, plays an influential role in our lives with both negative and positive impacts, including in the context of cultural differences.

Which brings us back to Herouxville. There's some evidence that one of the town councillors, a strong anti-immigration activist named André Drouin, played a leadership role in drumming up support for the charter—and likely, fear. Drouin, the key spokesperson on behalf of Herouxville regarding this issue, has been known to speak bluntly, referring to multi-culturalism as "idiocy" and demanding a moratorium on immigration to Canada.[26] He was responsible for drafting the controversial legislation, and has asserted that he brought this issue forward for the other decision makers to consider after eight years of planning. In a 2011 interview, he claimed to

THE POWER BEHIND HEROUXVILLE'S CHARTER?

André Drouin became the spokesperson for Herouxville regarding its charter and during its controversial time in the media. A retired military man, his background on these issues includes self-claimed ties to unnamed European groups, which, he asserted, conducted a multiyear "benchmarking analysis study . . . covering 19 countries," that concluded multiculturalism and accommodations to immigrants were tools to "transform a democracy into a theocracy." In a 2011 interview posted on an anti-immigration website, he boasted that the infamous town charter was eight years in the making, and done as a case study for this shadowy network that he claimed to be a part of.

Source:

Canadian Immigrant Report, "CIReport.ca Interviews: André Drouin," www.cireport.ca, Sept 16, 2011.

belong to a shadowy international "network" for which Herouxville served as a case study of an anti-immigration strategy.[27] (For more details, see sidebar: The Power behind Herouxville's Charter?)

Drouin's anti-immigrant bias was accompanied by great passion and purpose. Given that he had a significant leadership role—he was an elected town official, after all—it wouldn't be outrageous to suggest that he may have played a prominent role in creating Herouxville's fearful and defensive *tilt away* posture that resulted in the unusual code of conduct.

In the absence of Drouin, it's not unfair to ask whether such a town charter would have been created at all. Did it truly represent the feelings of residents in the first place? Or was it the result of emotional contagion from a highly charged, fearful leader with a few allies and a political agenda, who served as the emotional guide for the community? There is some evidence to suggest that the charter may have been unrepresentative.

In 2013, a reporter from a national newspaper returned to Herouxville to ask residents how they felt about the Quebec's proposed Charter of Values, which seemed to be inspired by their own town charter from six years earlier. Given that this town and its residents were considered the Quebec heartland and most likely to support aggressive assimilation laws, the results were surprisingly split.

Although many did approve of the province's proposal, others felt that, in banning public servants like doctors or teachers from wearing headgear such as hijabs or turbans, it went too far. In the words of one of the residents, "We're in the countryside and, it's true, we're not used to head scarves. But if you're a good nurse, that's what counts. It's not a turban or veil that says whether you're competent, it's what's underneath."[28]

Emotional Triggers:
The Role of the Amygdala and Limbic System

To understand emotions and their origins, we need to back up a bit and revisit the brain. It's believed that our brain evolved in stages, resulting in three distinct sections known as the reptilian, limbic, and neocortex. From an evolutionary perspective, the reptilian brain is the oldest and most primitive part of us. It regulates our automatic functions such as breathing, heart rate, startle function, swallowing, and a host of other tasks that are essential to basic survival.[29]

The next region in line to develop was the limbic brain, a feature we share developmentally with other mammals. This part of our brain is responsible for the "share and care" parts of our personality. It is critical for nurturing and defending our young, communicating vocally, play, community, empathy, and socialization.

The youngest brain region to develop was our neocortex.[30] This is the metaphorical home of our conscious mind. Thinking, attention, abstract reasoning, fine motor skills, and language are rooted here. The prefrontal cortex, the section encased by our forehead and behind the eyes, is particularly important. It is believed to be the brain area that determines our capacities for emotional intelligence.[31] The prefrontal cortex is responsible for a variety of executive functions including setting goals, planning, directing action, and guiding as well as inhibiting emotions.

The home base for emotions is in the limbic region. This part of the midbrain houses many structures including the amygdala, which constantly scans for threats and is the trigger point for the body's fight-flight-freeze mechanism.[32] Rick Hanson describes the amygdala hub succinctly:

> Moment to moment, the amygdala spotlights what's relevant and important to you: what's pleasant and unpleasant, what's an opportunity and what's a threat. It also shapes and shades your perceptions, appraisals of situations, attributions of intentions of others, and judgements. It exerts these influences largely outside of your awareness, which increases their power since they operate out of sight.[33]

A perceived threat by the amygdala can set off the body's fight-flight-freeze mechanism. The automatic response easily overpowers the thinking part of our brain. In this state, we become very reactive. This can work in our favour and help us, for example, jump out of harm's way (from a snake, say). But it also has drawbacks. For example, the amygdala can misfire when we interact with those who are different than us. It has been shown to be activated when we relate to those of a different race, suggesting that a potential cascade of unconscious feelings and bias are also at play in racial interactions.[34]

Our built-in negativity bias is accompanied by feelings of anxiety. These feelings, in turn, keep the brain scanning for threats, amplifying other unpleasant feelings such as anger, guilt, shame, depression, or sorrow.[35] Because we don't seem to have an equally strong automated response mechanism for positive inputs, we have to work harder to keep track of the good things. The result is a tendency to judge members of other racial groups unfairly.

In short, when dealing with those we perceive as "not us," thinking frequently takes a backseat to feeling. Especially if the situation involves uncertainty, confusion, or anxiety. Overactive amygdala responses, fed by Drouin's fears, likely played a role with the council members of Herouxville.

And why wouldn't they? With the events of 9/11, the so-called war on terror, and related propaganda as a backdrop, media stereotypes of Muslim peoples as dangerous, backwards, democracy-hating, fanatical, and violent have been prolific. With stories like that about a group of people who are religious, cultural, and ethnic outsiders, how could the emotional cores of Herouxville town councillors—like those of the rest of the Western world—*not* be overactive?

The feeling response makes it easier to put all Muslims (and similar immigrants) into the mental categories of "potential threat," "terrorist sympathizer," "female-hating," and "barbaric." Developing a town charter to protect your community, therefore, could seem like a rational choice, even when there's no evidence that the threat is at your town borders.

And this is why emotional literacy skills are so important to issues of diversity and difference. If we do not develop these skills intentionally, we risk living our lives on autopilot, our choices and behaviours governed by unconscious habits.[36] And when on autopilot, we may default to using the most readily available stereotypes thereby living in a state of guardedness and suspicion. We tilt away rather than towards those different than ourselves.

It's Hard to Talk about Diversity

Given how emotions impact human interactions and intergroup dynamics, it's not that surprising to find that even talking about our differences is challenging, especially in public. This struggle was well illustrated during a professional development session I co-facilitated. The daylong session, with a group of 150 high-performing young public servants, was not about discrimination or diversity, but rather about the importance of professional networking.

After an activity in which participants individually mapped out their networks and discussed their results with a partner, one of my co-facilitators asked: "How diverse was your network?"

The question was met with an incredible silence.

The facilitator repeated the question—and again, there was silence. This was in stark contrast to other questions asked that day, which had resulted in plenty of responses and participation.

At the end of the session, our facilitator team analyzed what had happened at that moment. It came as a great surprise because, overall, the participants were very talkative, quite diverse, and relatively young. If anyone might have engaged the question of diversity with ease and proficiency, this group was a likely candidate. However, they seemed to collectively freeze up, and our team wondered why. It was especially intriguing, as this public sector institution had been honoured with both diversity and best employer awards, indicators that many things were going well.

One of the facilitators, a twenty-year veteran of the company, responded very matter-of-factly: "Diversity is a very difficult subject in our organization—people feel as though they've done something wrong. This group of young people seemed to have picked up on this. It's like the subject is almost taboo."

Feelings of wrongdoing. Taboo. The words of the organization's veteran employee resonated strongly with my experience. That's how hard it has become to talk about these issues.

The challenges of plainly discussing issues of diversity and difference are not confined to a single organization or region. It is commonly accepted in this field that they are part of a broader social struggle in North America. As a result, the conversations are either avoided or come out in explosive ways.

It's not hard to understand why. After all, diversity and inclusion are about rectifying a problem. And the problem is not small. It goes beyond groups of people being left out. It includes ugly words (connected to strong emotions) like "discrimination" and "racism"—words that may evoke images of the Nazis and the Ku Klux Klan, and stories of helpless victims and brutal perpetrators. The content and context is fundamentally emotional in nature. So the feeling that individuals, groups, or organizations are doing something wrong is understandable. It is also one of the greatest challenges of doing this work.

Body Language: Our Early-Warning System

To state the obvious, emotions exist at both overt and covert levels. When we get angry, sad, or happy, the feeling has to break our particular personal threshold before we become aware of experiencing the emotion.[37] Before that threshold is reached, much of our feelings remain unconscious. And that's a problem, because without our full awareness those emotions influence our behaviour, thoughts, and choices.

But there is a way to get a jump on what's happening to us internally: to notice body language and tone of voice, both in ourselves and in others. The feelings we don't express overtly may be conveyed through our bodies. For example, researchers have known for some time that people express their bias regarding racial others by sitting further away from them, making less eye contact, and displaying increased facial muscle twitches. These signs indicate high levels of anxiety and nervousness.[38]

Unconscious body language is difficult to control. It may demonstrate our tendency to tilt away from (rather than towards) out-group members. Even actors—who are trained in the art of body language—are unable to hide their racial bias.

A 2009 study led by Max Weisbuch from Tufts University in Massachusetts used popular TV shows to observe the body language of actors. The study found strong anti-black bias, even though the black and white characters in these dramas were social and economic peers.[39] Ten-second video clips were created with audio removed and one character ingeniously cropped out so that their race was not apparent. Viewing the clips, impartial observers found that positive body language—such as smiling, nodding, and leaning in when talking—was far less common when white actors interacted with their black rather than white counterparts. (For more details, see sidebar: Body Language Experts Foiled by Bias.)

Nalini Ambady, one of the co-authors, bluntly stated in an interview that black characters were "less liked non-verbally than white characters."[40]

Such negative feelings portrayed by the unconscious interaction between actors—which is a form of anti-black, pro-white bias—has a direct impact

BODY LANGUAGE EXPERTS FOILED BY BIAS

A study by Max Weisbuch, Kristin Pauker, and Nalini Ambady showed that even those experienced in the art of relaying emotions may betray their hidden emotional racial bias. The research team used TV clips to observe the body language of actors, and identified strong anti-black bias. Clips of eleven popular TV shows—including *House, CSI, Grey's Anatomy,* and *Scrubs*—were specifically selected because black and white characters were portrayed as social and intellectual peers.

University students who had not seen these episodes viewed ten-second clips of interactions between either two white characters or one white and one black character. Two modifications were made to the clips. First, there was no audio. Second, only one actor—always white—could be seen. The second actor was cropped out of the frame. Regarding the white character remaining on screen, the students were asked, "How much does this character like the character they're interacting with?"

The results were unanimous.

The student viewers (who were all white) were clear in their choices. When considering body language, the hidden black characters—in spite of similar social status—were less liked than the hidden white characters by a significant margin. (The student viewers were unaware that race was a factor in the study.) Smiling, nodding, leaning in when talking—all examples of positive body language—were far less common when white actors interacted with their (hidden) black rather than white counterparts.

Source:

Max Weisbuch, Kristin Pauker, and Nalini Ambady, "The Subtle Transmission of Race Bias via Televised Nonverbal Behavior," *Science* 326 (Dec. 2009), 1711–14.

on the rest of us. In another phase of the study, the authors found that viewers were negatively affected by what they were viewing. Watching such subtly pro-white clips from TV shows (normally formatted and appropriate characters visible) resulted in higher pro-white scores on tests that measure unconscious bias. Putting this impact into context, according to the study, the eleven TV shows had an average weekly audience of nine million Americans *each*. This hints at the enormous impact of media alone in reinforcing existing racial bias in all of our lives.

So what's going on? Why all this body language bias?

It's a stretch to believe that, across eleven different TV shows, directors overtly and consistently gave their white actors directions to single out their black peers for subtle negativity. That would be plain weird. But the researchers did indicate that they were uncertain whether the negative body language was scripted by directors, an innate reaction by white actors, or some combination of both.

My creative passion is filmmaking, and I'm aware that the actor's instrument is their body. Accessing unconscious reactions and emotions is the real craft behind the work. It wouldn't be difficult to argue that the study did reflect the unconscious pro-white bias that the actors held. And why shouldn't it?

Actors live in the same society as the rest of us. Their job is to express their unconscious feelings convincingly to create believable and real characters. As the next chapter will explore, we all possess unconscious bias. Anti-black prejudice, to a greater or lesser degree, has been widely absorbed by North Americans. It would make sense, then, that actors who are trained to unleash their unconscious through body language would more readily reveal such bias. These performers, in essence, serve as cultural mirrors. They reflect back something unpretty that exists inside all of us.

To manage rather than be controlled by our feelings, then, we need to develop an early-warning system to the emotions bubbling below the surface of awareness. Self-awareness is the tool required for such advanced detection, the foundation upon which all other inner skills are built.

Inner Skill 1: Self-Awareness

According the Michael Inzlicht, a neuroscientist at the University of Toronto Scarborough: "There is substantial evidence that those with more executive control are able to regulate their prejudiced responses. . . . People who are better able to focus their attention and manage their emotions tend to be people who are able to regulate their stereotyped associations."[41]

Executive control refers to the work of the prefrontal cortex, including planning, evaluating, thinking about ourselves, and impulse control. And executive control is premised on self-awareness, the starting point for inner skill development.[42]

Self-awareness starts with attentiveness to our own emotions and needs. It includes knowing our strengths and weaknesses, and having a strong sense of our worth and capabilities. It is the ability to self-reflect, follow our instincts and gut reactions, and be aware of the impact we have on others and the world around us (and of their impact on us).[43]

Even with a good handle on our conscious selves, it's the elusive unconscious parts that behave as personal blind spots. Learning to direct our focused attention to the internal workings of our mind is critical to living a life where our actions and choices are aligned with our values. Especially regarding issues of racial difference and diversity.

Researcher and psychiatrist Dan Siegel argues that developing such inner knowledge—what he calls *mindsight*—helps us "name and tame" our emotions, so that we know how and when to constructively process and express them.[44] It also helps us counter the sweeping emotional charges that underlie intergroup interactions, especially when there is competition or conflict. Such insights may have been useful to the leadership at Herouxville as they developed an unnecessarily inflammatory town charter in reaction to a perceived—but non-existent—threat of outsiders.

The most extensive process for developing self-awareness that I'm aware of also happens to be the second inner skill, mindfulness meditation. This technique offers simple exercises for the brain that include attention to breathing, body sensations, and relaxation.[45]

Inner Skill 2: Mindfulness Meditation

Prejudice and stereotypes, as we have seen, are simply neural habits. As such, they are subject to neuroplasticity: they are flexible and can be altered through conscious attention. Mindfulness meditation has been shown to help change negative habits of the mind. It is the tried and true method of over two millennia for improving our focused concentration.[46] It's a specific form of attention that emphasizes our here-and-now experience. Mindfulness meditation is about being aware of what is happening in both the mind and the body, without reacting or judging.

This Eastern contemplative tradition has spread across the Western world over the last several decades. It has been modified for use in a variety of non-religious settings, including health care, personal growth, general stress relief, and leadership development.[47]

In his book *Mindsight: The Science of Personal Transformation*, Dan Siegel discusses the many benefits of mindfulness meditation. It can enhance resilience—our ability to bounce back from hardships—helping us tilt towards rather than away from challenging situations and people.[48] Further, from a neuroscience perspective, studies on long-term meditators suggest that we can literally grow and thicken the fibres in our prefrontal cortex through mindfulness practices, thereby enhancing our cognitive and emotional capacities.[49]

There are many ways to learn more about mindfulness meditation. Resources by teachers such as Thich Nhat Hanh, Pema Chodron, and the Dalai Lama are readily available, and there are local practitioners in many small and large urban centres. The most rigorously tested technique I'm familiar with is the Mindfulness Stress Reduction Program developed by Jon Kabat-Zinn at the University of Massachusetts Medical School. Dr. Kabat-Zinn has written a number of books on the topic and has helped spread mindfulness across the health care sector.[50]

Other Strategies for Developing Self-Awareness

Many strategies besides meditation can also help us develop self-awareness. Although beyond the scope of this book, the following may offer some starting points:

- Notice your own body language and tone of voice at regular intervals during the day. Track especially what happens when you get anxious, uncertain, or upset (clenched fists, irregular breathing, obsessive behaviours or thoughts).

- Take three to five opportunities daily to notice the shifts in your emotional state. Develop a broader palette of words to describe primary feelings (anger, joy, fear) as well as secondary ones (envy, contentment, nervousness).
- Recognize what issues, people, and situations emotionally trigger you into a state of fight-flight-freeze, especially regarding issues of racial difference. Everyone goes somewhere emotionally off-centre when triggered—where do you go?
- Keep track of daily events in a journal. Review them over time to identify your patterns of choices, reactions, and behaviours.
- Get feedback from trusted others. Ask them specifically to help you consider perspectives that may be in your personal blind spot.

Questions to spark personal reflection regarding racial difference can also help enhance our self-awareness. The following sample questions are adapted from cultural proficiency educator Randall Lindsay and his colleagues:[51]

- To what social identity groups (including race, gender, class, sexual orientation, and ability) do I belong?
- How are institutions and organizations in this country influenced by the dominant ethno-racial culture?
- How has my race and identity helped or hindered my progress in society, in small or big ways?
- How does race and social identity help or hinder people in my organization?
- How does my perceived status based on social identity in an organization (or society at large) affect my behaviour and motivation to achieve? In general, how might perceived status affect behaviour and motivation to achieve?

It's not easy to confront parts of ourselves that we are less aware of or that are contradictory to our espoused values. It can fuel painful emotions such as guilt, shame, anger, or defensiveness. This is where Deep Diversity's compassionate approach becomes important. Self-compassion helps us observe ourselves with curiosity rather than judgment. It's the salve to lessen the painful sting of our mistakes so we don't beat ourselves up. Yet it still holds us accountable. Compassion is essential; without it, we may not be able to focus our attention long enough to learn about and unlearn some bad habits about relating to others.

Finally, the key to developing any skill is practice and repetition. Although this may seem obvious, it's still worth mentioning. Persevering is the hardest part of any habit breaking and forming process. If you're like me, it's an imperfect series of forward and backward steps. So, practise noticing your body language and breathing, even if there's a stretch of days in which you don't. Continue to ask yourself about the impact of your social identity on each situation, even if it's an afterthought. Practise. Rinse. Repeat. Do this until it becomes automatic.

Acknowledging this challenge from the onset may help us push through periods of inconsistency without getting demoralized. In this case, "fake it till you make it" is a completely acceptable principle. It may also be the most realistic path of learning for most of us.

Compassion and self-awareness are especially important in helping us uncover hidden prejudices. In the next chapter, we will explore the biases that exist within all of us, regardless of our good intentions or egalitarian leanings.

BIAS: PREJUDICE WITHOUT AWARENESS

A Flutter in the Chest

I HAD JUST FINISHED a meeting and was walking towards the subway. Although it was a little cool, I felt overdressed in my suit and overcoat. My briefcase weighed in my hand. I had recently left my public school teaching job to work independently, and this had been an important meeting that could develop into a longer-term diversity contract.

As I neared the subway entrance, somewhat lost in thought, a young woman approached me. "Do you know where the government offices are?" she demanded, in a flustered tone.

I didn't know but asked if she had an address. She rummaged around in her knapsack looking for it. She had lost her wallet the previous day, she fumed, and hated having to replace all of her identification, health, and credit cards.

When she pulled out a paper with the address, I didn't know what direction to point her in. The city block and the building in front of us were so big that it was hard to tell whether the numbers were increasing or decreasing. But I offered to help her locate the office.

I did this for two reasons. I had some time on my hands, and mobility was an issue for her—she used a wheelchair.

She readily accepted my offer and we proceeded down the street together. We exchanged names and started talking. We hit if off immediately; within minutes, we were chatting like old friends. Natasha was witty, sarcastic, self-deprecating, and even a little flirtatious.

After we crossed a large intersection, she paused, looked me up and down, and stated with the utmost confidence, "Shakil—I bet you I know what you do for a living."

I had two conflicting thoughts: *How presumptive* and *I love her audacity!* This was completely in line with her gregarious personality, and part of why I instantly liked her so much. I was up for her little game. In fact, I felt that I had an ace up my sleeve, especially with the conservative suit and tie that I was sporting.

"Go ahead," I challenged. "Tell me what I do for a living."

Natasha scanned me again and pronounced, "You're either a psychologist, teacher, or social worker."

My jaw hit the ground. Besides the fact that I had just left teaching, if there were three professions that described the unusual job I'd created for myself, it would be those. I was flabbergasted. She looked on smugly as I affirmed that she had guessed right.

"Yeah," she continued, "from my experience, those are the type of people who stop to help strangers most often on a street . . . and on top of that, I'm a social worker!"

It was with this statement that I noticed a little flutter in my chest. This body twitch was subtle, yet important enough that I wanted to ignore it. It still evokes some shame to admit this, but I know exactly what that little flutter indicated. I did not expect her to say that she had a career as "elevated" and "respectable" as a social worker.

I expected less from her.

My surprise at her profession revealed something ugly in the depth of my unconscious: bias against someone in a wheelchair. Lower expectations of people with physical disabilities—it's called *ableism* and it's part of what I teach regarding diversity and inclusion. Am I not supposed to be the expert on these issues?

This form of unconscious prejudice—known in research terms as *implicit bias*—cares not if we are lay people or experts. We all have implicit biases; it's a part of being human. Such prejudice, hidden in the realm of the unconscious, influences our behaviour.

There is hope, though. Conscious effort can be applied to manage and reduce this masked form of bigotry that perpetuates feelings of "us" and "them."

Implicit Bias: Prejudice below the Radar

Deep within our subconscious, all of us harbor biases that we consciously abhor. And the worst part is: we act on them.

– Siri Carpenter, social psychologist[1]

The term *implicit bias* requires some work to understand fully. *Implicit* refers to "mental associations that are so well-established as to operate without awareness, without intention and without control."[2] In contrast, *explicit* feelings can be consciously detected, expressed directly, and publicly reported.[3] In the words of Mahzarin Banaji of Harvard University, a leading bias researcher:

> When we speak of implicit bias, we are talking about decisions that people make that are happening quite outside their conscious awareness but nevertheless have a systematic pattern to them. Those patterns tell us that they are using information about a person's group membership such as their ethnicity, gender, sexuality, religion, culture, or language—the list goes on.[4]

For the purpose of this book, I'll simplify matters and say that implicit bias is a hidden or unintentional preference for a particular group based on social identity such as race, gender, class, ability, or sexual orientation. It's a form of prejudice that is indirectly expressed, originating in the unconscious mind.

We hold beliefs about social groups at both visible and invisible levels of awareness. We commonly refer to these beliefs as *stereotypes*—generalizations about a group of people that can be based on a kernel of truth, an exaggerated reality, or even be an outright lie, resulting in the conscious or unconscious categorization of each member of that group without regard for individual differences. It's seeing someone as a symbol of a group rather than as an individual.

Some stereotypes are obvious and overt (such as Latin lovers, or women as homemakers versus men as money-makers). Implicit stereotypes, however, are subtler. They may be revealed through circumstances, when beliefs held below the radar of awareness are suddenly confronted. That's what happened in my interaction with Natasha. The low expectations I held of someone who used a wheelchair were uncovered.

Bias Helps: It's a Necessary Brain Function

It may surprise many of us to realize that implicit bias and stereotypes grow out of normal and necessary functions of the human brain. They are critical to how we perceive, categorize, remember, and learn about the world around us.[5]

The brain is a network of a hundred billion neurons, single cells that make up the majority of the nervous system. Neurons send and receive electrochemical signals to each other, creating networks and pathways that act as a high-powered communication system that allows us to regulate our bodies internally and react to our environments externally.[6]

From birth, we start developing neural networks for everything from recognizing speech patterns and forming our first words to learning to crawl, walk, read, or ride a bike. Our brains are associative by design. We learn by making connections between things, clumping, grouping, and pairing concepts. For example, most of us in North America have learned to make the following associations:

- ice cream with sweet (rather than savory)
- hammer with nail (not with cotton ball)
- snake with dangerous (not with cuddly)

Each of these pairings is a specific neural network. The stronger the association between two ideas is, the more well worn the neural path. In neuroscience terms, this is known as Hebb's Law: "neurons that fire together, wire together."[7] The more repeatedly we think, feel, or do the same thing, the more ingrained the neural path becomes. This, in essence, is called a *habit*.

The pairings or associations are learned from childhood, absorbed and shaped by the stated and unstated norms of our family, friends, and social and physical environment. This is a way in which we learn about our *culture*, a concept that encompasses any of the shared values, morals, behaviours, customs, and worldviews held by a large group of people. (Culture may often be more narrowly understood. For more detail, see sidebar: Defining *Culture*).

Another way to think about biases is as filters that help us pay attention to relevant stimuli while ignoring less important things. One scientific estimate suggests we may be exposed to close to eleven million pieces of information per second.[8] Take, for example, walking down a busy street. There is so much sensory information coming at us at any moment—cars, people, colours, temperature, awareness of social norms, odours, sounds, obstacles, and the comfort (or lack of comfort) of the clothing we are wearing, to name just a few.

If we were required to process and filter all that sensory information using the conscious mind, we would be utterly overwhelmed (and, likely, incapacitated). Anyone who drives a car, for example, may recall the nerve-wracking early stages of learning to navigate a two-ton mechanical beast through busy streets (see sidebar: Driving a Car).

Fortunately, this is one of the gifts of the unconscious mind—the ultimate multitasker. It processes vast amounts of information at lighting quick speed, categorizing, perceiving, remembering, and learning all at once. Comparatively, in conscious awareness, we can handle only about

DEFINING *CULTURE*

It's not unusual for people to wonder if multicultural nations like Canada or the United States have a culture, especially when contrasted to "Old World" countries like Italy, France, China, or India. The underlying assumption behind this question is a narrow definition of *culture* that includes only language, ethnicity, or national identities.

All humans not only have a culture, but we are also part of many cultures simultaneously. *Culture* encompasses all the learned patterns of behaviour, thinking, and being in the world that are passed down between generations (as opposed to genetic). In short, it's our "way of life." Culture includes values, morals, customs, foods, language, worldviews, priorities, beliefs, goals, as well as personal or professional boundaries.

Much of our culture, in fact, exists as a silent code, an unspoken understanding within a group of people. Our culture is not static, but continuously changes over time. It is altered in small or large ways with each generation.

There are also a large number of *subcultures*, groups that deviate in some small or large way from the main cultural group. Variations include, for example, regional differences (urban or rural), areas of work (corporate, public, or not-for-profit), or age (Boomers, Gen-X, or Millennials).

Sources:

J.N. Martin and T.K. Nakayama, *Experiencing Intercultural Communication: An Introduction* (New York, NY: McGraw-Hill, 2011), 32.

Michelle LeBaron and Venashiri Pillay, *Conflict across Cultures: A Unique Experience of Bridging Differences* (Boston: Intercultural Press, 2006), 14.

forty pieces of information at any one time. And we can only keep a handful of items in direct focus.[9]

Although the mechanism is not fully understood, Nobel laureate Daniel Kahneman and his collaborator, Amos Tversky, proposed the idea that humans have evolved mental shortcuts called *heuristics* to deal with the vast

DRIVING A CAR:
FROM CONSCIOUS STRUGGLE TO UNCONSCIOUS HABIT

When we start developing a new skill, the first days and weeks are usually filled with a certain amount of stress, anxiety, fear, and frustration, as we figure out how to do things.

For example, when learning to drive a car, we are taught to go through a number of steps before the car even moves. Seat belts on, adjust mirrors and sightlines, foot on the brake, one hand on the steering wheel and the other on the gear shift as we put the car into drive. At this stage, the conscious mind—which is not good at multitasking—is in control, generating stress in the process. This anxiety is amplified as we navigate traffic lights, change lanes, avoid hitting other cars, or watch for cyclists in our blind spot.

However, as the months and years pass, the task of driving becomes significantly easier, and the multitude of factors are effortlessly juggled and balanced. This happens because through repetition, our adaptive unconscious takes over. This part of our mind is exceptional at handling multiple tasks simultaneously. Once this transition from conscious to unconscious occurs, a new complex habit is formed, making whatever we are doing easy. This pattern applies to any learning process, whether it involves a sport, musical instrument, language, or area of expertise.

ocean of information to which we are exposed.[10] It is hypothesized that these neural codes enable quick, efficient judgments that assisted our ancestors to survive through the ability to rapidly distinguish, for example, friend from foe or snake from rope.

Such neurological shortcuts remain important today. They act as filters to keep out extraneous information and help us focus on what's really important. Our ability to differentiate which lane to keep our car in while we drive is a testament to this. So is our tendency to suddenly notice how many other people are wearing the same style of jacket that we just bought.

Heuristics are also believed to be the mechanism behind intuition, sometimes described as our sixth sense.[11]

The problem is that stereotypes and implicit biases are also forms of heuristics. That's when they hurt rather than help us.

Bias Hinders: It Distorts Our Worldview

As a result of . . . pre-established filters, we see things, hear things and interpret them differently than other people might. Or we might not even see them at all!
– Howard Ross, author and bias consultant[12]

Mental shortcuts about social groups create problems for us, because important information is usually filtered out. Howard Ross writes, "Our perceptive lens enables us to see certain things and miss others, depending on the focus of our unconscious. It filters the evidence that we collect, generally supporting our already held points of view and disproving points of view with which we disagree."[13] He correctly suggests that bias creates literal—not just metaphorical—filters, causing us to fixate on some things while ignoring others. Further, a quick-and-dirty heuristic in the form of stereotype or implicit bias about a social group can lead to misjudgments of people and situations, thereby threatening fairness and justice in day-to-day life. (See sidebar: Bias Threatens Fairness).

For example, commonly held stereotypes in our culture incorrectly support these associations:

- woman with frail or weak (not with chief financial officer)
- black man with criminal or athlete (not with engineer)
- immigrant with poor English (not with public relations expert)

Such neural associations follow the path of least resistance, quickly linking a group with a commonly held belief. Stereotypes, in essence, function as neurological imprints. Once the pathways are sufficiently reinforced, they are resistant to change.

BIAS THREATENS FAIRNESS

Researchers Mahzarin Banaji and R. Bhaskar describe memory and belief as generally operating outside awareness or conscious control, thereby posing a threat to fairness. They write:

"When stereotypes are unconsciously activated and used, two direct challenges to the implementation of fairness are posed: *a)* perceivers and targets are often unaware of the steady and continuous rendering of judgments and *b)* judgments are based on beliefs about targets' social groups rather than on targets' actions."

Much of this dynamic has to do with the rapid speed of the unconscious mind, which outpaces our ability to think about the situation. Our unconscious mind is "on" at all times. One of its jobs is to continually assess the world around us, making sense of what is happening in the external environment and looking out for threats. As a result, it continuously makes judgments on all things, including people. This can be beneficial, but if our bias has been activated, it can be harmful. Although both perceivers and targets may be aware of some judgments taking place, it is unlikely that either would be consciously aware of the degree of these judgments.

In addition, it's clear that biased judgments are based on beliefs about social groups rather than on their actual behaviours.

Source:

M.R. Banaji and R. Bhaskar, "Implicit Stereotypes and Memory: The Bounded Rationality of Social Beliefs," in *Memory, Brain and Belief*, ed. D.L. Schacter and E. Scarry (Cambridge, MA: Harvard University Press, 2000), 140.

Implicit Association Test: Measuring Our Bias

Considerable research on implicit bias has emerged from Project Implicit since the late 1990s. This project helps expand our understanding of prejudice and discrimination beyond the overt, obvious forms manifested through racial epithets, images of swastikas, or ideologies of segregation.

Project Implicit researchers created the Implicit Association Test (IAT), a free online assessment that asks participants to pair words with groups of people, measuring which associations most easily come to mind. Measured in milliseconds, the faster responses reflect stronger unconscious associations—stereotypes and intuitions. These associations reveal dimensions of prejudice that are better predictors of many behaviours than one's explicitly stated opinions.[14]

Various versions of the IAT have been available to the public online since 1998, and millions of people have participated in these tests. Hundreds of studies have also been conducted worldwide using the results.

The following are six key findings from Project Implicit:

- *We all have implicit biases.* Humans have unconscious preferences in everything from race, age, and gender to sexual orientation and class issues.[15] Such bias is described as "the well-learned and automatically activated associations between psychological qualities and social groups."[16] Family structures, peers, education, and other societal institutions reinforce cultural norms—many of which originate from arbitrary preferences. These norms benefit some groups while marginalizing others. As a result, we unconsciously prefer some groups to others.
- *We are unaware of our implicit biases.* Negative associations towards various social groups are harboured below the radar of consciousness. They exist as a "blind spot" in our awareness. People are therefore surprised to learn that they hold such biases.[17] Further, research demonstrates that many groups of people—including the researchers from Project Implicit themselves—can behave in contradiction to their stated beliefs. Bias becomes especially pronounced in decision-making situations where time is limited or stress is high. It is difficult to be aware of this implicit bias because it regularly outpaces our ability to think about it.[18]
- *People differ in levels of implicit bias.* In relationship to a particular social category, we can possess high, medium, or low/no levels

of implicit bias. A person may demonstrate low bias regarding race and high bias in another category, such as sexual orientation. Various factors, including the influences of family, culture, and social context, influence the level of bias in an individual and in a category.[19]

- *Implicit biases predict behaviour.* Studies consistently demonstrate that implicit measures of prejudice on the IAT are a far better predictor of our choices and behaviours regarding social groups than what we believe, say, feel, or think about ourselves explicitly.[20] These hidden biases frequently cause us to incorrectly and unjustly judge people. This ranges from simple acts of kindness to more consequential decisions such as who is interviewed for a job or given life-saving drugs. We give those who are most like us the benefit of the doubt, while we are harsher towards those not like us, especially if they are from minority groups. And the IAT scores better predict what we will actually do in the future than what we think we may do.

- *Group power buffers or magnifies bias.* Although all of us possess unconscious prejudice, the negative effects of bias are linked to social power and group status in society. There are high-status or dominant groups (whites, men, heterosexuals, educated, rich, able-bodied) and low-status groups (racialized/Aboriginal, women, LGBTQ, working class, people with disabilities). High-status groups demonstrate greater favouritism towards themselves and higher implicit prejudice towards non-dominant groups. In fact, there's a tendency for low-status groups to also unconsciously favour dominant groups. Overall, non-dominant groups predominantly feel the impact of bias, whereas dominant groups are buffered by greater social capital.[21] (We will return to the theme of power in chapters 5 and 6.)

- *Minority groups internalize negative bias.* Unconscious prejudice can erode both trust in and desire to be with our own ethnocultural or racial groups, especially if our identities are non-dominant and lower status. Patterns in studies consistently show that both high- and low-rank groups hold more implicit prejudice towards minority group members. For example, one sampling of 260,000 race IATs conducted over a nineteen-month period demonstrated that it was not only whites who demonstrated a strong pro-white bias. Latinos and Asians exhibited equally strong pro-white biases.[22] Other evidence suggests that even when members of a minority group explicitly state that they prefer people of their own race, their implicit choices and behaviours show the opposite—that they, in fact, favour the dominant group.[23]

The IATs yield significant evidence that is difficult to deny. Millions of people have been tested, and the sample sizes are so large that the results cannot be dismissed as random. In the words of the researchers: "Hundreds of studies show that implicit attitude measures are stable over time, internally consistent, and reliably predict related judgments and behaviors, including political attitudes, voting, academic achievement scores, consumer preferences, social evaluation, hiring decisions, and verbal and non-verbal affiliation."[24]

One reason that the IAT is such an effective tool is that what it measures, our unconscious prejudice, is consistent and difficult "to deliberately modulate, control, or fake."

Beyond the Lab: The Real-World Effects of Bias

To make the implicit bias results more connected to the real world, consider examples from a few social domains: the workplace, health, policing, and education.

Workplace Recruitment: What's in a Name?

A 2009 University of British Columbia study conducted by Philip Oreopolous analyzed the response of employers in the Greater Toronto Area to 6,000 mock resumés for jobs across twenty occupational categories, including marketing, financial, programming, and retail.[25] The mock resumés had similar qualifications, with one key difference: some candidates were given typically English-sounding names like Greg Johnson and Emily Brown, while others had "foreign-sounding" names like May Kumar, Dong Liu, and Fatima Sheikh.

The results were surprising for many. The resumés with English-sounding names had a 40 per cent higher rate of callbacks for interviews, compared to resumés with the same education and job experience but with names that were Indian, Chinese, or Pakistani (the three ethnic groups of focus in the study).

Such results can occur even when companies are actively looking for diverse candidates. In a 2004 resumé study from the United States that focused on white-sounding and black-sounding names (such as Tyrone, Leticia, and Jamal), pre-interviews with companies indicated that they were "hungry" for qualified racial minority candidates.[26] However, the resumés of white-sounding names still triggered 50 per cent more callbacks than resumés with black-sounding names. Even more shocking, lower-skilled white candidates received considerably more interview callbacks than higher-skilled black candidates.

Health Care

A 2007 study in the context of health care involved 220 internal medicine and emergency room doctors from Boston, Massachusetts, and Atlanta, Georgia. They were required to assess a hypothetical male patient showing symptoms of a heart attack.[27] All of the physicians were presented with the same patient profile, the only difference being the accompanying photos: they were either of a black man or a white man, both middle-aged. The doctors were also given a race-based IAT as well as questionnaire that determined their explicit attitudes towards race. The researchers wanted to know whether race played any part in the doctors' assessment of the patients, specifically as to whether to provide thrombolysis, an anti-clotting therapy for heart attacks.

Although the physicians reported no explicit preference for black or white patients, the IAT (the black-white race test) demonstrated something different. The doctors—like any random group—fell into three distinct categories of unconscious racial bias: low, moderate, and high. The doctors who tested with high levels of anti-black bias were much less likely to give the life-saving anti-clotting drugs (the correct procedure based on the patient symptoms) to black patients.

The results of this study, unfortunately, are not isolated to a lab test. It is widely known in medical research that whites are twice as likely as blacks to receive thrombolytic therapy for heart attacks. Blacks are underprescribed these life-saving drugs; this statistic was part of the impetus of the research, conducted by Dr. Alexander Green and colleagues.[28]

Furthermore, such practices are not uncommon in the health care context.[29] A 2002 study called "Unequal Treatment" by the Institute of Medicine in Washington, DC, found significant evidence that discrimination played a role in the differential treatment of racial minority and Aboriginal patients compared to white patients—ranging from physical exams and history taking to referrals for advanced treatment required for diseases like cancer.[30]

Racial Profiling in Policing

Studies have also shown that individuals with higher levels of anti-black bias are much more likely to mistake day-to-day items such as a wallet or cell phone for a weapon when it is in the hands of a black person rather than a white one.[31] Known as *weapons bias*, this is another focus of implicit race bias, especially in the context of the policing. Bias researcher Mahzarin Banaji and law professor Curtis Hardin reviewed over two dozen experiments on weapons bias and found the results consistent.[32]

To illustrate, participants were shown a series of images and instructed to quickly "shoot" if the person is armed and "don't shoot" if the person is unarmed. The results were predictable: participants were more likely to confuse harmless things like a camera or soda can for a weapon when held by a black person and therefore "shoot" these unarmed people. However, participants were more accurate when viewing images of white people in the same circumstances, resulting in significantly fewer unarmed whites being shot. These results are, unfortunately, similar for not just whites taking such tests but also for Asians, Hispanics, and even blacks. This demonstrates how minority groups who are the targets of such bias also internalize negative beliefs. Further, the results are similar among professional police officers. Banaji and Hardin bluntly state: "Such findings have important implications for police officers given the broader finding that police consistently use greater lethal and non-lethal force against non-white suspects than white suspects."

Bias in Learning: Stereotype Lift and Threat

A growing body of research demonstrates that implicit associations in the form of stereotypes are powerful enough to create self-fulfilling consequences in learning and education.[33] Individuals can live up or down to stereotype lift or stereotype threat, respectively. Here are some examples.

In a groundbreaking study conducted at Stanford University in the mid-1990s by Claude Steele and Joshua Aronson, high-achieving African-American students took the Graduate Record Examinations (GRE). The control group took the GRE under neutral conditions, while the second test group was told that the GRE was an intelligence test. Test group 2 did considerably worse than the control group. Researchers concluded that the stereotype threat—based on the incorrect belief that blacks are psychologically inferior to other groups—was so powerful unconsciously that it caused the lower scores.[34]

Another study went a couple of steps further, focusing on East Asian women and their relationship to stereotypes regarding mathematics. When the generalization that "women are worse at math than men" was introduced, the test scores for those East Asian women were significantly lower than for the control group of East Asian women who were not primed with the stereotype. However, when the stereotype that "East Asians are generally better at math than other groups" was evoked, the scores were higher than in the control group, with gender "threat" disappearing. These results demonstrate stereotype threat and lift, respectively.[35]

To explore how much effect exists outside the classroom in a broader context of learning, another study focused on white golfers who were told

POSITIVE STEREOTYPES ARE ALSO HARMFUL

It is important to note that regardless of stereotype lift or threat, generalizations limit human potential and so should not be used. Negative stereotypes—the more obvious type—can be painful, reduce performance, and limit one's sense of self.

Positive stereotypes, however, are equally limiting. They box people into a small reality of who they are "supposed to be" according to others, rather than who they actually are according to themselves. In this way, individuals can be hampered from truly exploring their human potential. This is a loss for themselves and for the workplace (or other) environment.

Although stereotype lift is used in the context of studies to understand human behaviour, it should never be used in an attempt to increase performance in a workplace or in society broadly. On the contrary, it would be highly unethical to do so.

they were being compared to black golfers. (In reality, there was no black group.) When told that the research was focused on which racial group possessed "natural athletic ability," the white golfers did worse than the control group who were given no generalization (demonstrating stereotype threat). When the white participants were told that the study was to determine which racial group had the greater strategy and golf "intelligence," their scores improved significantly (demonstrating stereotype lift). This study verified the continued existence of the historically incorrect belief that whites are intellectually superior, while blacks are naturally athletic.

Overall, such studies provide ample evidence that unconscious generalizations are pervasive in all aspects of our lives, not just in the academic setting.[36] Regardless of lift or threat, however, stereotypes do more harm than good. They limit human potential. (See sidebar: Postive Stereotypes Are Also Harmful.)

Bias: Nature or Nurture?

An ongoing debate is whether prejudice is ingrained in our biology or the result of our culture and society. Is Us versus Them a matter of nature or nurture?

The research suggests that it's a bit of both, but in surprising ways that many of us may not have considered. In short, we are born with the bias hardware, while society provides us with the software.[37]

There is significant evidence that implicit bias has a neurological base, with the roots of "us" and "them" firmly set in unconscious processing. Various studies show that when faces of people of other races are flashed so quickly on a screen in front of us that conscious awareness is impossible, the threat response of the amygdala is still activated. Other research suggests that our attention—indicated by electrical activity in the brain— commonly prioritizes those of our own race. And our behaviour regulation centres become more active when we are being politically correct and fearful of making mistakes. (For more details, see sidebar: Us/Them Rooted in Brain Structures.)

These results are seen as early as the first year of our lives. A 2012 University of Massachusetts Amherst study demonstrated that even nine-month-old infants respond more quickly to people of the race of their caregivers than to others. The newborns were able to match emotional sounds with facial expressions faster and differentiate more rapidly between faces of their own race.[38] Before five months of age, however, babies respond to different groups in a more or less similar manner.[39] Other preferences are also established within this short time period, including greater responsiveness to the gender, language, and accents of the primary caregivers.[40] So, although we may be born prejudice-free, we learn bias at a very early stage. This suggests that we come pre-equipped with some neural mechanisms that seek to define and identify members of our own tribe.

Why? Again, some researchers point to evolution to help us understand our reaction to group differences.[41] It is suggested that our cave-dwelling ancestors needed to know instantly who was part of the tribe and who was

US/THEM ROOTED IN BRAIN STRUCTURES

The following research highlights how racial responses have their basis in unconscious processing:

- Race perception begins with face perception, as early as one-tenth of a second after encountering another's image (Ito and Bartholow). Our amygdala, the structure that monitors for threats, is more active when we encounter faces of members of other racial groups (also known as out-groups). In test situations using photographs, blood-oxygen responses in the amygdala were activated even when the faces of other-race people were flashed so quickly that conscious awareness was not possible (Ronquillo et al.).

- The prefrontal cortex and anterior cingulate cortex—structures related to evaluation, monitoring, and behavioural regulation—are activated when we are being careful not to make racial mistakes (that is, being politically conscious or correct). Many studies show that these regions are stimulated when participants experience conflict between their egalitarian beliefs and their automatic negative responses to members of other racial groups (Ito and Bartholow).

- A series of brainwaves—called by names such as N100, N200, P200, and P300—are shown to be linked to a variety of racially based reactions. These reactions include greater wariness of those not like us, greater attention to in-group members (those most like us), and our degree of motivation to update information about out-group members (Ito and Bartholow). In short, electrical activity in the brain shows that we have different responses to those whom we perceive as racially "us" and "them."

Sources:

Tiffany A. Ito and Bruce D. Bartholow, "The Neural Correlates of Race," *Trends in Cognitive Sciences* 13,12 (2009), 524–30.

Jaclyn Ronquillo et al., "The Effects of Skin Tone on Race-Related Amygdala Activity: An fMRI Investigation," *Social Cognitive Affective Neuroscience* 2 (2007), 39–44.

not. To mistake a foe for a friend may have cost them their lives. It would have been an advantage to be neurologically wired with an "alliance detection system" to instantly recognize a tribe member and react swiftly with fight or flight.[42] From this perspective, we are the progeny of those who were hypervigilant and survived. Our ancestors are those who preferred to err on the side of caution and mistake (and mistreat) a few friends as enemies, rather than risk being those who were mistreated.

When examined as a whole, it appears that part of our biology causes us to tilt away from—rather than towards—those we perceive as different than ourselves. I was floored to learn this. It went against my long-held belief that socialization was the only force to consider. But the hardware we come with seems to matter in ways I'd never contemplated.

Now, as the research on babies reveals, who gets defined as "us" *is* learned from exposure and experience from all our spheres of contact. The software is determined by our culture and context. The upcoming chapters on tribes and power will explore in greater depth the roles of socialization and systemic discrimination in establishing social norms. But suffice it to say that both nature and nurture have a significant place in forming unconscious bias, stereotypes, and racial intuition.[43]

It's important to state, though, that although the hardware may not be changeable, there's evidence that the software is.

Bias Reduction Strategies

In 2007, the results of my first IAT on race revealed that I had a *moderate* preference for white people over black. I felt embarrassed and devastated. As someone who works in the field of diversity and prejudice reduction, this was a significant result that led to some profound reflection. Part of me wondered if I should quit my day job. I sat with the results for many months, thinking about their implications for my work.

My results, however, did make some kind of sense. On a personal level, they fit my earlier life story. I am of South Asian ethnicity, and I grew up in small-town Canada. Part of me wanted to be white. I worked hard to assimilate and "fit in." On a broader, societal level, pro-white pref-erence is part of the collective North American story. As Project Implicit research demonstrates, the majority of both white and non-white people have pro-white bias. We've all drunk from the same cultural punch bowl, and our tongues are stained similar colours.

So, what to do? I started by doing what I knew best—I asked questions, I read, I sought out new research and revisited studies addressing implicit bias. I found evidence that although implicit bias is consistent over time and rooted in unconscious processes, it is not completely fixed. That means we can change it. I was struck by the simplicity of one particular approach developed by researcher Brandon Stewart. He instructed study partici-pants to use a counter-stereotype—specifically, the word "safe"—when-ever they encountered a black person, and found a reduction in anti-black prejudice.[44]

Given what I was learning about how the brain works, Stewart's strat-egy made sense. If stereotypes are simply an overused neural pathway—with the association between black people and danger being particularly entrenched in our minds—then just telling myself to not make the associa-tion would likely fail. Stewart's strategy suggested that I needed to build a new neural pathway by creating a new association between black and posi-tive qualities.

Over the next few years, I began a simple experiment with myself, usu-ally when I was riding the subway. Public transit allows natural time and space to people-watch. Taking advantage of the opportunity, whenever I saw black people in the subway car, I would close my eyes and intentionally make a positive association: *kind, generous, philosophical, hard-working, engi-neer*. I repeated the words to myself several times while trying to picture the person's face with my eyes closed. Tackling my own anti-black bias became a mini-habit, a regular way to pass a minute or three of my time.

In November 2012, five years after I took my first IAT, I repeated the process. This time, the results indicated that I had "little to no automatic preference between white people and black people," the lowest level of the IAT. Although it's far from a scientific conclusion, I credit the method inspired by Stewart's research for helping reduce my anti-black bias.

While I adopted this method, I was also conscious of three things. First, that I was attempting to broaden the number of overall possible categories of black people in my mind, with an emphasis on increasing my list of positive, non-stereotypical associations. (There are also positive stereotypes of blacks: athletic, cool, good dancers, and so on).

Second, that black people are just another human group and so should not be romanticized as possessing only "good" qualities. (I did not, however, actively work to increase my negative list of qualities—society has done that adequately for us all.) But the awareness is important that within all our groups—within all individuals, really—exist the range and potential for a multitude of positive and negative human qualities.

And finally, that this process is awful to describe and may be painful for many of us to read. For that I am deeply sorry. I find it beyond deplorable that, in this day and age, members of our human tribe would be described as "unsafe," as somehow "less than," because of an arbitrary measure such as skin colour or ethnicity.

The criticism may also be levelled that to "gaze" at another person for our own learning in this manner is distasteful, perhaps even dehumanizing. And there is validity to such a critique. The thing is, it's happening all the time regardless. Recall that our unconscious mind absorbs information from our surroundings, tracking information that reinforces bias and stereotypes. So, do we want to do it unconsciously with a negative collective outcome or positively for a mutually beneficial outcome? It's a less-than-ideal choice, but choose we must. By guiding our conscious attention, we may be able to undo the unconscious habits of mind that hinder fairness between individuals and groups.

This strategy, known as counter-stereotypes, is one of many promising prejudice reduction strategies that researchers have shown can reduce bias. I'll highlight seven strategies that can help minimize such prejudice and its impacts.

1. *Role models:* Various studies have shown that seeing people representing groups targeted by negative stereotypes in a positive light reduces bias. For example, exposure to strong, positive models

such as Barack Obama and Oprah Winfrey or Canadians Naheed Nenshi and Michaëlle Jean helps reduce bias, as does reading about the historical contributions made to civilization by Muslim-Arab communities.[45] Another study found that students in prejudice reduction classes taught by black professors showed a greater decrease in both implicit and explicit bias at the end of term than those in a similar class taught by white professors. (Similarly, female engineering students had more positive implicit attitudes towards math when taught by female professors than when taught by male teachers.)

2. *Inner motivation:* Research has found that people with an inner drive to be non-prejudiced are less biased. Bias researcher Michael Inzlicht has found that those who are intrinsically motivated (that is, who believe that both they and society are better off with less prejudice) tend to be more successful in bias reduction efforts than if the motivation is externally driven (they are pressured to comply).[46] Studies have also found that those with strong logic skills and willpower are able to better achieve their prejudice reduction goals, because they are able to notice their preferences and curb their judgments about others.[47]

3. *Noticing personal contradictions:* All of us display inconsistencies, to a greater or lesser degree, between our stated beliefs and how we act. Studies show that people who are able to detect the contradiction between their intentions and actions are more successful in reducing bias.[48] Meditators are especially good at this. Their mindfulness training teaches them to observe their thoughts and feelings without judgment, a technique that tacitly familiarizes one with such discrepancies.[49]

4. *Intergroup contact and friendships:* Exposure to people different than ourselves helps curb the impacts of implicit prejudice.[50] Such bias was reduced among white college students if they were randomly assigned a black roommate rather than a white one. Friendships between Muslims and Christians in Lebanon as well as between blacks and whites

in Chicago were found to improve implicit attitudes. In a U.K. study, implicit prejudice was found to be lower between white/British and South Asian/British children to the extent that they reported friendships. In an extension of this study, bias reduction occurred even among children who had no friendships outside their own racial group themselves but reported having friends who did.

5. *Counter-stereotype plans:* A substantial body of research demonstrates that using counter-stereotypes can help.[51] Brandon Stewart, as discussed above, instructed study participants to simply use words like "safe" whenever they encountered a black face, and found a reduction in anti-black prejudice. The key to this subtle reminder is that participants themselves create both an intention and a plan to tackle bias.[52] The stereotype, although not eliminated by this method, is diminished in impact because now another positive association is created in the subject's brain, which may become more automatic over time. It is important to maintain an awareness, though, that all groups have both positive and negative qualities. Attempting to paint a group as only positive is not only unrealistic but difficult for our conscious mind to accept.[53]

6. *Carrots and curiosity:* Because a stereotype is a generalization, when we encounter a member of a racial group different than our own, there is a tendency for our brain to register that person as a symbol of the group, rather than seeing them as an individual. (This does not happen for members of our own group.)[54] Researchers have found that getting subjects to ask simple questions about vegetable preferences (as in, I wonder if this person likes carrots?) helps in bias reduction. It appears that the power of curiosity can help humanize others, so that we see them as unique individuals rather than as representatives of a group.[55]

7. *Education and training:* Various types of diversity trainings may have various results. But specific strategies, such as those listed here, have been shown to reduce bias in the long term. Patricia Devine and her colleagues at the University of Wisconsin worked with ninety-one

non-black students on the impersonal and implicit nature of bias and provided flexible strategies (including many listed here) to "break the prejudice habit." Over 90 per cent of this group had a pro-white bias, as measured by the IAT, at the start of the study. After the education interventions, the results of the IAT showed a strong drop in implicit attitudes, results that lasted up to twelve weeks after the training.[56]

Inner Skill 3: Self-Regulation

All of these bias reduction strategies are premised on the first inner skill, self-awareness, and are greatly supported through practice of the second, mindfulness meditation. However, attunement to our feelings, needs, motivations, and behaviours is insufficient on its own to break our prejudice habits. Self-regulation is needed to manage the difficult feelings that emerge from uncovering bias.

We are learning through our mistakes, which can make us feel bad. This is not an easy process. According to Michael Inzlicht:

> Errors, fundamentally, are an adverse experience, an emotional experience. People don't like them, they don't want to make them. They sweat more, there's heart rate acceleration, pupil dilation, release of cortisol. . . . It turns out the errors are really important in establishing self-control. People who are sensitive to the errors they make—who react and adapt to the mistakes they make—are really good at self-control and executive functions.[57]

Inzlicht suggests that if we listen to what our negative feelings have to tell us regarding our own prejudice and stereotypes, we can exert greater self-control.

Self-regulation (sometimes called self-management) is the third inner skill required for navigating emotionally loaded terrain and reducing bias.[58]

Self-regulation is the capacity to keep disruptive emotions and impulses under control, especially under stress. It's the ability to own our mistakes rather than avoiding them. Self-regulation includes having optimism, being able to experience positive emotions, and behaving with integrity and in socially desirable ways. It also includes knowing how and when to acknowledge and communicate important feelings, rather than simply repressing them. Self-regulation has been described as the inner skill that "frees us from being a prisoner of our feelings."[59]

In my encounter with Natasha, I could have ignored the flutter in my chest that indicated I had made a negative assumption about her skills and capacities. But I noticed it (self-awareness) and reflected on the experience. I tilted towards rather than away from my mistake, which required managing feelings about being "bad."

My inner critic can be harsh and loud, and my journey has been to learn from my errors without beating myself up. (Others, however, may be on the opposite end of the spectrum. They may need to learn to listen more closely to their inner critic and take responsibility.) Integrating compassion has been a key aspect of my own self-regulation practice. So has understanding that much of what we struggle with is a normal part of the brain's architecture. Together, these insights allowed me to implement the subway strategy to reduce my anti-black bias.

Whether we have named them or not, all of us have developed some practices to help us manage our emotions through difficult situations. We know that such strategies make us feel better, even if only temporarily. We may, for example, know that going for a walk helps us cool down after an argument. For some of us, venting to a confidant is useful, or writing in a journal. Constructive regulation strategies help us put things into perspective, problem solve, and recover from or prevent difficult emotional situations. Some strategies, however—such as smoking, binging on food or alcohol, obsessively ruminating, or worrying—may be less constructive.

Jan Johnson from Learning in Action Technologies, a teacher who introduced me to emotional intelligence work, compiled a useful list of positive, neutral, and negative strategies. (See sidebar: Self-Regulation Strategies.)

SELF-REGULATION STRATEGIES

Positive (or Neutral*) Strategies
Breathing/relaxing consciously
Exercise and eating well
Noticing own body sensations
Self-expression (art, music, dance, etc.)
Laughing, telling jokes
Positive self-talk
Curiosity to ask questions and learn
Moving towards the relationship rather than away

Negative (or Neutral*) Strategies
Addictions of all kinds
High-risk behaviours
Self-imposed isolation (not knowing how to reach out)
Negative self-talk
Self-sabotage
Dismiss the other person
Withdraw or walk away
Want to blame, sabotage, or hurt others
Feelings of shame (excessive)
Feel powerless to make changes in the relationship

*Some strategies in low doses may have a net effect that is negligible.

Source:

Jan Johnson, "Self-Regulation Strategies—Methods for Managing Myself," Learning in Action Technologies, www.learninginaction.com.

Many resources and supports are available on self-regulation, as well as a significant body of work. The following questions may serve as useful starting points:

- What are common things that regularly cause me emotional stress? Consider home, work, family, finances, and so on.
- What strategies (positive or negative) do I use to de-stress? Consider both low-intensity and high-intensity situations or conflict.
- What do I do to prevent difficult emotional circumstances that appear regularly in my life?
- What emotional situations trigger my fight-flight-freeze response, and how do I deal with these? Once off-balance, how do I recover?

For self-regulation in the context of bias and racial differences, consider the following:

- What feelings emerge when I consider the possibility that I have biases and have likely acted on them, whether consciously or unconsciously?
- What was my response when I was corrected by someone for something I said about issues of difference (or when I was accused of being prejudiced)? What were my feelings? (If I haven't experienced such an accusation, how might I feel and react?)
- What issues about social identity (such as race, gender, or sexual orientation) am I most comfortable talking about? least comfortable? Why are some easier than others?
- How often do I engage in conversations about race and difference that challenge and extend me beyond my comfort zone?
- What other self-regulation strategies might help me learn more about my own biases?

The more tools we develop to manage ourselves, the more effective we can be in learning and unlearning biases, and having critical conversations about our differences.

Although there may be bias towards dominant group members such as men, white people, heterosexuals, rich people, or abled-bodied people, the negative impact of prejudice tends to affect non-dominant groups—women, racialized and Aboriginal people, LGBTQ people, poor people, and people with disabilities. As we will see in the next chapter, being part of the dominant group comes with social power, an invisible cultural momentum that supports us whether we are aware of it or not. This sets up the historical challenge facing society today, of good-hearted, well-intentioned people on both the giving and receiving end of prejudice struggling to work through our differences.

In the next part of the Deep Diversity framework, we will explore the effect on human behaviour of belonging to tribes.

4

TRIBES: BELONGING DRIVES HUMAN BEHAVIOUR

A Fish Tale

THE PROVINCE I live in is blessed with freshwater lakes both large and small. On a drive with a friend through one of the pretty, pastoral towns outside of Toronto, I was struck by an unusual sight. On a pier extending into Lake Ontario were more than a dozen fishermen, all East Asian in ethnicity. Given that these small towns are predominantly white, the men on the pier really stood out. Amid snacks, hot drinks, and camaraderie, the anglers skilfully pulled some healthy-sized trout from the water. We started chatting with one of the guys and learned that they were from Toronto. This was their weekly adventure.

I left that interaction with a feeling of wonder. How much things had changed in the province since my childhood. I grew up in small towns like these, and—besides me and my family—it was a rarity to see racialized people fishing. They were certainly not seen in such large numbers. On top of that, these guys fished weekly! Amazing how much the demographics and lifestyles had changed.

This gentle but important act of cultural integration filled me with hope and encouragement. Fish-loving cultures from the East meet angling towns from the West. What a great milestone! That was about a year before I heard of the term *nipper-tipping*.

What's that, you ask?

Well, imagine for a moment a man with his thirteen-year-old son fishing peacefully on the shore of a picturesque lake. The careful lesson of attaching a hook to the line. Bait wriggling in little hands. Fish tales from the past, transferring learning from elder to child. And some quiet moments in between.

Incidentally, the ethnicity of this pair is East Asian. And that's a factor as they are approached by two white men, locals who accost them. Threats and accusations are uttered at the father-son team, who are confused and fearful. The scene escalates and the thirteen-year-old is grabbed and, in front of his shocked father, harshly pushed into the lake.

This is a sad but true example of nipper-tipping, a term that combines a racial slur against East Asians with the sophomoric prank of "cow tipping." (Supposedly, bored youth seek thrills by tipping over cows that sleep standing up.)[1] On the surface, it seems almost cartoonish and therefore hard to take seriously.

Except that these were racially charged incidents. They came with ethnic slurs and verbal harassment, as well as physical intimidation and violence. Over a period of a few years, property damage and physical assaults became commonplace. One violent incident put a young man into a coma, resulting in permanent brain damage.

Assaults on people of East Asian descent while fishing became a flashpoint in Ontario in 2007. The issue attracted national media coverage, and the Ontario Human Rights Commission (OHRC) launched a preliminary inquiry to understand the nature and extent of the phenomenon.[2] The common factors were that the locations were small towns within a two- to three-hour drive of Toronto, the hobby was fishing, the targets were always East Asians (and their friends), and the perpetrators were locals who were white.

There has been much commentary on this issue, tending to fall within three broad categories. Some say that this is an example of outright racism and the narrow-mindedness of small-town white people. Or that East

Asian Canadians were not following appropriate fishing rules and so have brought this situation onto themselves. Lastly, that this behaviour stems from competition for dwindling resources, limited space, and declining fish stocks.[3]

Although each of these elements has some relevance, I'd like to look at the phenomenon from a broader framework. This situation exemplifies the third component of the unconscious mind—the human tendency to protect the interests of our own tribe and its members, regardless of whether we are white, black, brown, or otherwise. Before we can try to undo the negative impacts of our group-ish nature, such as prejudice and racism, we need to explore how deep its biological and cultural roots go.

Tribes Are Rooted in the Brain

We fear what our ancestral history has prepared us to fear . . .
snakes, spiders and humans from outside our tribe.
— David Myers, professor of psychology[4]

We have an inherent tendency, called *risk intuition*, to assess threats in our environment. According to David Myers of Hope College in Michigan, psychological science has identified an important factor that feeds our risk intuition: interacting with those not from our "tribe." It is theorized that risk intuition was a survival mechanism that allowed early humans to quickly distinguish a tribe member from an outsider—and a threat.

As we saw in the previous chapter, we learn to tune in to the race of those closest to us starting in the first year of life. With repetition, neural networks form and create racial imprints, so to speak. Our brains don't have to work as hard when confronted with those most like us. This allows a sense of ease and comfort, because the job is being handled by our unconscious.

This Us/Them formatting of our neural wiring happens quietly and automatically deep inside the brain, without needing of overt encouragement. (Recall, from chapter 1, the drinking water study.) Without our conscious awareness, our brains are constantly signalling feelings such as greater trust or empathy for strangers who share certain racial features with us.

If other races do not play a major part in our day-to-day existence, neural pathways countering these early imprints do not form. The brain also has a "use it or lose it" rule—unused neurons are pruned away for the sake of neural efficiency.[5] The cumulative effect of genetics and socialization is the forming of our unconscious racial habits and norms.

Race Is Science Fiction

Having said that, the concept of racial tribes is rooted in society rather than in biology.

Race is a social construct; it's a concept created by people rather than something genetic in nature. Science long ago proved there is only one race—the human race—and that there is more genetic variance within a group than between groups. (See sidebar: Race Is Social, Not Biological.) Although there may be apparent differences between groups along the lines of skin colour and other physical characteristics, extending this principle to imply that there are separate races is a dubious pseudo-science at best.

Yet, on a day-to-day basis, race matters, whether we agree with the concept or not. So it must be treated as though it were real. Author and academic Robert Jensen captures its complicated nature: "Race is a fiction we must never accept. Race is a fact we must never forget."[6]

Tribes are even more complicated than race. Our sense of belonging to a group includes a broader range of socially important identities. They include gender, class, sexual orientation, age, religion, language group, and ability. Our sense of tribe can also change according to context and circumstance. In the workplace, interdepartmental rivalries can boost performance through micro-group identities (such as sales team A is outperforming sales team B). A national identity may suddenly become a point of group pride and celebration during global competitions such as the world cup of soccer or the Olympics.

But when we get too invested in an identity, tribes can also limit co-operation and positive outcomes. Sports fans can become unruly when their team loses or wins, and clash with opposing fans or police. Racial

RACE IS SOCIAL, NOT BIOLOGICAL

The concept of *race* is complicated. Science has shown that there are no distinct races based on biological differences, that in fact, we are one human race. The concept of race, then, referring to different human groups with supposedly distinct physical characteristics, has been created by people. It is a social construct with no real scientific basis. The colour of one's skin, which is simply caused by cell pigmentation, is a microscopic genetic variable. A black person and a white person, for example, may be closer genetically than two white people or two black people.

When considering differences between groups of people, it is more accurate to discuss *ethnicity*—a shared identity based on cultural, linguistic, religious, historical, and/or racial factors (Pakistani, British, Somali, Jewish, and so on).

While we know that race is a social construct, it still matters in today's society. So race also needs to be treated as though it were real.

It is because of the social construction of race that the term *racialized* has gained traction in academic and activist circles. But this word, too, is imperfect, as it's not difficult to argue that all of us, including white people, are racialized. The reality is that all terms are problematic, so for accessibility, in this book I've used *racialized* interchangeably with other common terms such as *non-white*, *person of colour*, or *racial minority*.

Source:

American Anthropological Association, "Statement on 'Race,'" www.aaanet.org, May 17, 1998.

identities can also lead to violence and negative feelings, as the East Asian fishing confrontations demonstrate. History teaches us that when intergroup tensions escalate to the extreme, the atrocities of genocide become possible, as demonstrated by Rwanda, Bosnia, Nazi Germany, and the historical attempts to exterminate Aboriginal peoples across the Americas.

Social scientists have studied the dynamics of groups, identity, and belonging for decades. Their findings have been synthesized into a framework called social identity theory. This theory is an evidence-based lens that is useful when attempting to understand the complicated dynamics of discrimination and racism in our organizations, as well as in society at large.

Tribes Are Created by Culture

We generally are not highly aware of the rules of the game being played, but we behave as though there was a general agreement on the rules.
– William Gudykunst, professor of human communications studies[7]

My nephew Zephan lives around the corner from me. When he was about three years old, we developed a little ritual whenever I passed by his daycare. If I happened to walk by when the children were out for recess, he would rush to the fence. I would crouch at his eye level and visit for a couple of minutes, me on one side of the fence and him on the other. Just before I'd leave, he would give me a happy little kiss through the bars. It truly made my day.

Then one time, I leaned towards the bar for our ritual kiss only to have Zephan pull back and gleefully yell, "*No* kissy!" I felt a surge of confusion and hurt. I also saw that a number of his little friends were standing behind him watching, including a couple of older boys. This was the last day he kissed me in front of his daycare friends.

I later heard from my sister about Zephan's newfound conviction that "boys didn't kiss." For a short while, he even resisted kissing his mother. He was not taught this at home or by his daycare providers. We suspected that he had picked it up in the social context of his daycare peer group. Current research supports the suspicion about the formation of Zephan's gender identity, that children are influenced strongly by the gender "club" of their peers.[8] Although our peers are a significant part of the process, they aren't the only factor. It's deeper than just socialization; the process involves internal mechanisms that seek to define who and what we are.

Social identity theory explores these dynamics between individuals—their identity and behaviour—in relationship to social groups. Pioneered by Henri Tajfel and John Turner, this body of work has developed through decades of research from around the world that have uncovered patterns that are common in human group behaviour.[9]

It is widely accepted in research that belonging to groups is a key driver of human behaviour, both on conscious and unconscious levels. Fundamentally, membership in a tribe helps us make sense of our place in the world. It removes ambiguity about others and ourselves.

An individual's self-concept—who we are—is derived from a combination of how we perceive ourselves in specific situations and our sense of belonging to various groups. These might be broad groups in society or specific ones in the workplace. And we frequently experience a tension between our need to belong and our desire to be seen as unique.

Our tribal identities are also heavily influenced by culture, all those ways of being, thinking, and acting that we learn from our environment. William Gudykunst, a scholar of multicultural communications, described culture also as a shared understanding of the "rules of the game" that emerges in an unstated manner and is specific to each context; it is commonalities among relatively large groups of people.[10] We unconsciously learn these rules from a variety of channels including family, peers, media, schools, and society at large. As this happens, the role of groups in our lives becomes more entrenched in how we view ourselves, solidifying our sense of self. Hence, my nephew Zephan and his daycare friends.

Belonging to social groups is an important part of our self-concept. Value and emotions are associated with such membership.[11] Our sense of gender, for example, begins very early. Many toddlers in the Western world, like my nephew, learn a number of gender rules by age three. For example, they learn that wearing a dress is "only for girls," as is the colour pink. Our unconscious is easily trained by our environment, as it absorbs the lessons and stitches together mental shortcuts about what is and is not "normal." Our interactions with our peer groups, family, community, and media immerse us into the norms and rules. They become an implicit part of who we are and how we make sense of others in the world around us.

If asked, for example, why dresses and pink are only for girls, our conscious mind will justify our behaviour. It will find a reason even when there is little rationale, biological or functional, for such clothing or colour segregation. Fundamentally, it boils down to a sense that the choices "feel" right to us. Although this is learned behaviour—not all cultures share the aversion to males wearing a flowing, one-piece garment that extends down the legs—the feelings seem tied to neural architecture that demands that our tribal identities be defined.

Even within the same culture, what feels right changes over time. In the North American/European context over a hundred years ago, pink was considered the more decisive, strong colour and given to boys, while blue was for girls. In fact, at the time, all children regardless of sex wore dresses till about age six because they were considered the most practical.[12]

In-groups and Out-groups

Our social identity—including race, gender, class, and sexual orientation—is that part of our self-concept that derives from belonging to social groups. It's also tied to the identification of *in-groups* and *out-groups*, people whom we perceive to be similar or dissimilar to ourselves. Social identity theory can help us understand the complex intergroup dynamics and social alliances underpinning racial controversies such as the Asian angler issue in small-town Ontario.

In-groups: Those Like Us

In-groups are people most like us. We care about our in-group and are taught to socialize with people from this group. We share the same references as to what is "normal" in communications and interactions. We unconsciously understand the unstated rules of the game. We are more willing to make sacrifices for our in-group and we do not always require equitable return from them. We tend towards generosity and a willingness to overlook mistakes made by members of our in-group.

Our alertness to our in-group can be subtle yet powerful. For example, I find my radar sensitive to noticing strangers who share my South Asian ethnicity. My Jewish friends have commented on a similar awareness of those like themselves, as have friends who are gay. Each group playfully refers to such heightened awareness as "Jew-dar" and "gay-dar," respectively.

Besides such socially important identities, in-groups can be more fleeting and arbitrary. They can be based on the city you live in, the sports you play, or whether a researcher places you randomly on a blue or green team during an experiment. The results seem to be fairly consistent. There is a natural tendency to feel good about our in-groups, creating a positive sense of identity. This result is the formation of an *in-group bias*, which is especially pronounced if we belong to high-status groups in society.

The neurological underpinning of tribes makes it easier to appreciate why we notice and prefer our in-group members, especially those tied to key social identities. Through a lifetime of being immersed in specific cultural patterns, the result is strong, unconscious neural imprints—we just intuitively sense what normal behaviour is. Efficiency is a key design element of neural circuits. The less our conscious mind is needed, the less energy is required to handle the task. This same neural efficiency results in less awareness and therefore less control over some behaviours, actions, and choices.

Out-groups: Those Not Like Us

In contrast, out-groups are people we view as different than ourselves. Because we have not been taught to socialize with members of out-groups, we may feel uncomfortable in their presence. Out-group members are perceived as "all the same," whereas it's easier to recognize the nuances between individuals within our in-group.

Facial features are a classic example. If we haven't been socialized in an environment with East Asian people, it may be difficult for us to see the differences between those of Vietnamese, Chinese, or Japanese ethnicity, for example, let alone recognize the nuances within an ethnic group. If we haven't taken conscious advantage of our neuroplasticity, our neural networks are likely not refined enough to tell the difference, and so "they all look the same."

The rules for social interactions and relationships may feel less clear with out-group members, creating conscious or unconscious anxiety. Our unconscious processes, which look for familiar patterns, struggle to comprehend out-group behaviours and environments. The conscious mind has to be more engaged, which requires greater energy and effort. If you've ever travelled to a new country where both language and customs are unfamiliar, you may have experienced this effect.

As a result, there is a tendency for greater frustration and confusion in communications with out-group members, and our unconscious mind's desire to avoid out-groups is usually high. Everything is more work when engaging with out-group members. This means we already feel under stress, so we are harsher in our judgments, we are less forgiving, and we expect more in return from out-groups.

Why? Because social norms are emotionally loaded and out-group behaviour disrupts our sense of what's normal. A substantial body of research shows that most social norms only become visible when they are breached by out-group behaviour. (See sidebar: Breaking Social Norms to Make Them Visible.) Out-groups behave in a way that inherently breaks accepted social norms, and this experience is emotional, especially for the in-group.

Take, for example, the handshake—an innocuous cultural tradition in North America. A "good" handshake occurs with bodies about two to three feet apart; it requires a firm grip with three up-and-down motions as well as eye contact. I remember learning early in my socialization that a firm handshake was especially expected of men, whereas women could get away with something softer (though less so in a workplace context). I remember learning that a weak handshake by a man was not okay (out-group behaviour); it was "girlie."

Of course, this is purely context-specific. Cultures across the world have traditions such as greeting with kisses on the cheek, like in Persian or Dutch cultures, or the lack of eye contact that signifies respect in many Asian traditions. In some conservative interpretations of Islam or Judaism, respect is also shown by not shaking hands or making physical contact with

BREAKING SOCIAL NORMS TO MAKE THEM VISIBLE

Through observational studies, theorists such as Harold Garfinkel have demonstrated that many social norms and practices (background expectancies) are taken for granted. They become visible only when they are broken. People use background expectations to participate in everyday interactions such as taking one's place in line, offering a certain amount of space during a conversation, or boarding a bus and sitting on a seat. People often perform these "mundane" tasks without question, and only become aware of them when norms are violated or "breached." As Garfinkel demonstrated, making the commonplace scenes visible reveals them. A person may feel uncomfortable if a stranger stands too close to them during a conversation. People will be irritated and maybe even angry if one skips a line and walks to the front.

Breaching experiments, which disrupt normal routines, illuminate the taken-for-granted practices. In one breaching study, students pretended to be boarders in their own home. Parents reacted by trying to make sense of the peculiar behaviour and demanding an explanation. In another example, Stanley Milgram studied responses to intrusions in subway lines. The concept of a lineup, or queue, can vary depending on culture, so they offer a "window" into how different cultures may interpret a social situation differently. People usually responded to intrusions in the line through corrective and defensive reactions to maintain the line's integrity. The practice of queuing becomes visible when someone breaks the rules; then people attempt to act to restore order.

Sources:

Harold Garfinkel, *Studies in Ethnomethodology* (Polity Press, 1991), 36–37.

Stanley Milgram et al., "Response to Intrusion into Waiting Lines," *Journal of Personality and Social Psychology* 51,4 (1986), 683–89.

George Ritzer, *Ethnomethodology in Sociological Theory*, 8th ed. (New York, NY: McGraw-Hill, 2011), 397–98.

non-family members of the opposite sex. Post-9/11, the simple handshake became a flashpoint for anti-religious emotions. Many people, including politicians on both sides of the Atlantic, were offended when conservative Muslims or Jews refused to shake hands with members of the opposite sex.[13]

So social norms that are usually invisible can, when they are broken, become the source of controversy and emotions. Perhaps this, too, was an evolutionary adaptation that helped keep tribe members in line when the size of group was extremely small. But it is less useful in a global village.

In the fishing story that began this chapter, the in-group/out-group dynamic is demonstrated by the violent reaction of the local white fishermen towards the Asian anglers. To break this down further:

- The victims would identify with the *East Asian in-group*. From this perspective, the out-group consists of the local whites.
- The perpetrators are part of the *White in-group (local)*. From this perspective, the out-group includes the anglers of East Asian ethnicity.
- A few of the victims were also white, because they were friends of the East Asian Canadian anglers. They, however, might be described as part of the *White friends of East Asian anglers in-group*. Their out-group would also include the local whites, even though they all belong to the broader white in-group of society.
- Remarkably, both victims and perpetrators have a social identity in common: they would identify with the *Angler in-group*. Anyone who does not identify with the hobby of fishing would be part of the out-group.

So, in-groups and out-groups are defined from the perspective of the individual (and group), and the concepts are very relative. We all simultaneously occupy a variety of in-groups and, therefore, out-groups. But one crucial aspect of the Asian angler story will be taken up more completely in the next chapter: power.

DOMINANT AND NON-DOMINANT GROUPS

We all belong to groups that are in-groups or out-groups relative to each other. It is when the power dynamic comes into play that an in-group becomes a dominant group. The following examples illustrate a number of higher-status groups that hold cultural and institutional power:

- *Gender*: Men are the most powerful gender in-group in North America and in the world, dominating decision-making and leadership positions across societal institutions (government, big business, media, police, and so on). From this perspective, women and transgender people are non-dominant or minority groups.
- *Race*: The members of the dominant racial in-group in North America share common white-European ethnicities, and control the levers of decision making across the corporate, public, and not-for-profit sectors. Racialized and Aboriginal people, who are non-dominant, are proportionally under-represented in the spheres of social power. (It wouldn't be difficult to argue that white people are the dominant racial group globally, in spite of smaller numbers compared to their racialized and Aboriginal counterparts.)
- *Ability*: Able-bodied people are the dominant group nationally and globally; societies are designed to meet their needs almost exclusively. Much less social consideration is given to people with disabilities, who occupy a non-dominant or minority status.
- *Sexual orientation*: Heterosexuals form the most powerful in-group with regard to sexual orientation. People of diverse sexualities are part of the out-group.
- *Class*: The dominant in-group with regard to income includes middle- to upper-class earners. Working-class and poor people are part of the economic out-group.

Source:

Lopez and Thomas, *Dancing on Live Embers*, 263–72.

Dominant and Non-dominant Groups: The Imbalance of Power

The relative social power of the groups in the story affects the way it is told and understood. But not all in-groups hold equal status and power in society—a crucial point in understanding the intergroup dynamics.

For historical socio-economic and political reasons—conflict, colonization, cultural or religious norms, and so on—there are always high-status and low-status (or dominant and non-dominant) groups in society. Taking power into account helps us more fully discuss the interplay of tribes and racial dynamics in the fishing controversy. (See sidebar: Dominant and Non-dominant Groups.)

How Tribes Played Out in the Asian Anglers Controversy

The dominant in-group in the region where most of the Asian angler incidents took place—as it is in the nation—is white. In this area, racialized and Aboriginal people make up less than 4 per cent of the population.[14] The targeted out-group was the anglers of East Asian ethnicity.

An inquiry launched by the Ontario Human Rights Commission into this issue drew attention to a contextual factor: there was competition for limited space and resources. Over time, it had become more difficult to find spaces for fishing and other leisure activities on public places along waterways, such as piers, docks, and bridges.[15]

It's likely that the white angler population of that region felt the competition for space more acutely than other groups. More people of all backgrounds started to find their way to fishing holes that had previously been frequented only by locals. However, the focus of the dominant in-group fell on the most obvious out-group—East Asian Canadians—rather than on other white people, outsiders who were less recognizable as such.

The OHRC report emphasized this point:

Being highly visible as presumed "outsiders", the activities of Asian Canadians may also be subject to greater scrutiny than others. For example, submissions raising concerns about the practices of Asian

Canadian anglers frequently cited a single incident, often several years in the past, as the basis for sweeping negative statements about the Asian Canadian angling community as a whole.[16]

Earlier in this chapter, we noted that a group already under stress judges out-groups more harshly. In-group bias (those well-worn neural pathways) results in greater alertness and criticism of out-group members; the perception of their missteps is more pronounced. The inquiry found that locals were quick to generalize negatively. One local concluded that Asians had no respect for Canada after witnessing one occurrence of an Asian Canadian angler leaving garbage behind. Another local stood firm in his accusation that "Asians are raping our lakes," after witnessing a single incident of an Asian Canadian keeping undersized fish.

The OHRC found that some local whites expressed overt hostility towards Asian Canadians by "drawing a distinction between 'Asians' and 'Canadians', and expressing opinions that 'Asians' 'keep everything that they catch' . . . [that they] 'have a reputation for cheating', and have a 'cultural disrespect for Canada's laws and decency standards'."

The inquiry also found that there was no evidence of any one group violating laws more than another. The psychology of the dynamics of groups is such that even if a white angler left garbage behind or poached fish illegally, there would be more leniency towards the in-group member, with no (or low) resulting consequences. The report noted there were no incidents of non-local whites being harassed or attacked for fishing in the same manner as the East Asian Canadian anglers (unless they were perceived as friends of this racial out-group). In the words of the inquiry:

> There are individuals within every community who do not follow the rules, are inconsiderate towards others, or break the laws. . . . What is of concern is when Asian Canadian anglers, as visible outsiders in relatively homogeneous communities, are subjected to disproportionate scrutiny, and assumed to be more likely than other Canadians to be breaking the laws, with the result that all Asian Canadian anglers are then viewed or treated in a hostile manner.

Most white locals who made formal submissions to the inquiry focused on the fishing practices of the Asian Canadians and denied that race was a factor. This is another manifestation of in-group bias—we are quick to point out missteps and errors of out-group members to explain escalating tensions and assaults. In essence, out-groups are not only the targets of in-group threats and assaults, but are also responsible for the violence that happens to them.

Notice that the white people in the story call themselves, and get to be called, "Canadians," while the Asian Canadians need some hyphenation or qualification, or are even described by locals as "non-Canadians." This is the power of the dominant in-group: to define itself as normal, see itself with pride, and perceive and define all other groups in contrast, usually as competitors or threats.

This power to define "normal" is one of those systemic powers, usually invisible to the dominant group itself. Invisible, but not without consequences. It's devastating to realize that being white makes one more likely to get appropriate emergency room treatment, or that having an Anglo-sounding name makes one 40 to 50 per cent more likely to get a job interview. It's an invisible advantage, a momentum constantly working in favour of the dominant group, that influences cultural and institutional norms and values.[17]

That dominant group bias moves easily from generalizations and incorrect beliefs to outright hostility towards out-group members is well illustrated in the case of contested space for anglers. But similar things happen all over the world. In this story, it's about the dominant white in-group literally attempting to push out the Asian Canadian out-group in the context of fishing in southern Ontario. In Myanmar (formerly Burma), it's the Buddhist majority retaliating against a Muslim minority.[18] In Pakistan, it's the Sunni Muslim in-group who legally are allowed to persecute the Ahmadi Muslim out-group.[19] Taken to the extreme, genocide is the ultimate demonstration of violent in-group bias. The 1994 Rwandan genocide was perpetrated by the Hutu majority against the Tutsi minority.[20]

Inner Skill 4: Empathy

Categorizing is normal human behaviour. So is a tendency towards anxiety and autopilot when dealing with new and challenging situations involving out-group members.[21] But unconscious bias and stereotypes are destructive, especially as they impact historically non-dominant groups. So what can be done about the tendency to categorize? How do we reduce the Us/Them tendency that seems influenced by both genes and culture?

Empathy is a good starting point.

Empathy is the ability to tune in to the emotions of others, perceiving their feelings, needs, perspectives, and concerns. Although we can never truly "know" another person's experience, nor actually "walk a mile in their shoes," empathy will take us a fair distance down that road. Empathetic people are regarded as excellent in meeting the needs of others, in their personal or professional lives.

Emotions expert Daniel Goleman describes empathy as follows:

> a critical skill for both getting along with diverse workmates and doing business with people from other cultures . . . [where] dialogue can easily lead to miscues and misunderstandings. Empathy is an antidote that attunes people to subtleties in body language, or allows them to hear the emotional message beneath the words.[22]

Developing empathy for others is intimately linked to the inner skills of self-awareness and self-regulation. As the following example demonstrates, we can be ambushed by the Us/Them tendency in subtle and unexpected ways. But training to catch ourselves in the act may be helpful in expanding the circle of "we."

We Couldn't See Eye to Eye

I was having a hard time focusing during a lunch-and-learn session on fundraising for the office charity. There was something odd about the mannerisms of the manager, Giselle, who was presenting. It was her eyes—they seemed almost closed the entire time she spoke to our group of thirty staff. Although Giselle held her head up and smiled in a friendly manner, her eyes seemed to be looking directly down at her feet.

It was very off-putting, at least for me.

Watching her, I began to feel uncomfortable and even a little agitated. Many thoughts rushed through my head: *Is she aware she's looking down so much? I wonder if others have noticed? Of course they have! How could they not? Surely she must know—someone must have given her feedback on this before they promoted her to manager status. Should I talk to her afterwards? Is it my place to?* And so on . . .

I became aware of my inner chatter and discomfort. So I took a breath and started sorting through my feelings. I became aware that I felt embarrassed *for* her, and that my feelings were strong enough that part of me wanted to leave the presentation. Her unusual mannerism was causing me to subtly tilt away from her. I also noticed the desire to turn to the person next to me and gossip about what we were witnessing.

Instead, I paused and noticed what was happening in my body. To myself, I quietly named the discomfort, as well as the desire to leave and to gossip. Doing this self-reflection somehow helped me shift gears. It allowed me to become curious about myself as well as Giselle.

I realized something: closing her eyes during a presentation was out-group behaviour. She was breaking the social norm of what I considered a "good presentation." And as discussed, someone breaking a social norm can be a very emotional experience.

I further reflected on my previous interactions with this manager. During my consultancy in this large accounting firm, I had talked to her a few times. She had avoided making eye contact during our conversations, too. I was, however, unaware of how severe it was until she was in front of the group.

Then it struck me: perhaps she was really nervous and extremely shy.

I hadn't considered this before, because my feelings of discomfort had overpowered my ability to think. This understanding helped me move past her out-group behaviour and open the door further to empathy. *In spite of her shyness, she's giving a presentation in front of a group. She's pushing herself into things that are difficult for her? Okay—that's gutsy.* Feelings of admiration, understanding, and compassion now mixed in, muting the discomfort I originally felt.

I remember looking around the audience to see how others were reacting to Giselle. I did a quick scan of body language and found little that gave away how anyone else was feeling. This was normally a very pleasant staff team, cordial and friendly and, true to form, they appeared to be listening attentively.

Perhaps it was just me? The presentation ended and we all went our separate ways.

In a conversation with a couple of staff on a later day, Giselle's name happened to come up. An instant reaction popped like the top of an overshaken bottle of soda: "She is so weird! Her eyes were closed the whole time!" said one, referring to the presentation. The other responded, "I thought maybe she was blind—I really did! How did she become a manager? Isn't speaking in front of others part of the job?"

Clearly I was not the only one who had noticed her out-group behaviour. I was also quite certain that their charged comments specifically stemmed from Giselle's presentation. She was new and they did not work with her directly. "I think she's painfully shy" was all I offered, in a non-judgmental manner.

"Oh," responded the first person, whose face and tone softened. Apparently that hadn't been considered. The second person mumbled something and turned away. Although I can't be certain of the exact impact, their body language suggested that my words altered something internally. I believe Giselle went from being someone "weird," whose behaviour seemed difficult to understand or predict, to being "shy," a state her colleagues could better relate to and empathize with.

If the reaction of discomfort I shared with these two colleagues was an indicator, Giselle had been cast into an out-group based on "preferred body language during presentations." All three of us had in common a pile of feelings about Giselle that had led to an immediate negative judgment of her as a person. The important difference was that I had caught myself in the act of ungenerous thoughts and feelings, and so was able to shift something internally (and, perhaps, for the other two as well).

As it's said, if you name it, you tame it. By noticing what's happening to us, our thinking mind is engaged. This can take some steam out of unconscious processes that push us towards behaving less generously. Curiosity can help foster understanding—both in ourselves and others—and empathy can lead to a deeper acceptance of differences, especially when interacting with out-group members.

Tools for Cultivating Empathy

Researchers C. Daniel Batson and Nadia Y. Ahmad from the University of Kansas have found that empathy can be developed through a variety of methods, including the following:[23]

- media such as books, TV, movies, or internet sources that offer perspectives of those different than ourselves
- intercultural dialogues between conflicting groups, as well as peace camps and personal storytelling opportunities
- discrimination-simulation activities that allow participants to experience a role that is marginalized
- specific educational programs designed to enhance positive feelings towards others

Cultivating empathy starts with deep listening skills and curiosity, both for us and for the person or group with whom we are interacting. I've found the following questions offer a starting point on the empathy pathway:

- How well am I listening to what the other person or group is saying?
- What are the feelings underneath the words being said?
- What emotions and judgments am I experiencing as I listen? (Name them.) How might these feelings and reactions be getting in the way of really understanding what's being said?
- How might it feel to be in their position, under their circumstances? What might they be needing or feeling right now?

More specifically regarding race and difference, the following questions may be useful, especially when interacting with out-group members:

- What social identities—theirs and mine—may be at play in the interaction?
- Is there an interplay in this situation between dominant and non-dominant identities? How might this help or hinder the communication?
- If the person or people are part of my out-group, how might that be limiting what is being heard or interpreted, by them or by me?
- Can I catch myself in the act of bias, assumptions, or stereotypes during this interaction?
- How might my lack of historical knowledge facing this group be getting in the way of understanding the person, group, or issue? Have I named this lack?
- What is their experience of me at the moment (how I'm listening and what I'm saying)?
- What respectful questions can I ask to better understand the person, group, issue, and circumstances?
- What might it be like to walk in this person's shoes for a day?

Empathy functions in tandem with other inner skills such as self-awareness, meditation, and self-regulation. Studies have shown that those who can more accurately assess sensations within their own bodies—such as feeling our heart rate—are also more accurate at sensing what is happening for others emotionally.[24] And greater awareness of what happens in our bodies is a key part of the practice of mindful meditation. Further, enabling the power of curiosity requires self-regulation, especially if the interaction is emotional in nature.

The overlap and linkages between inner skills are also the key to unlocking the final unconscious dimension in the Deep Diversity framework: power.

POWER:
THE DIVIDING FORCE

Marco's Rebellion

MARCO began to hate the police. Again, they had pulled him out of his community and embarrassed him in front of his peers. The last couple of times, it was for minor infringements like stepping outside the town's boundary and mouthing off. I wondered what he would do this time.

Jail would be another round of humiliation. Last time he had broken out and made a mess of things, running through the three neighbouring communities yelling about conspiracies and injustice. Many people didn't even look up. He was ignored.

Part of me felt bad for him. He had no idea of the extent of the prejudice or how significantly the odds were stacked against him.

Next, the police conducted a "search and seizure" in Marco's community, following up on rumours that drugs were being sold openly. Residents were made to stand like criminals, watching while law enforcement agents ransacked their meagre buildings and homes. This after they had just rebuilt from flash floods.

Yet again, most people from the neighbouring groups didn't even look up. Marco and his community, Orangevale, were once again ignored.

Marco and the Orangevale residents were getting seriously demoralized. I could see a sense of helplessness setting in. Marco would soon have others join him in his rebellion. Then things would really get chaotic.

The results are consistent. I know. I've done this many times.

This is the City Game, an experiential activity we use in our leadership programs to teach about the distribution of social power in society. We explore the concepts of *privilege*—unearned advantage or status based on one's identity—and its opposite, *marginalization*—disadvantage, or low status based on identity. I've conducted it at least two dozen times in five different countries with young adults aged seventeen to twenty-four, and the results are always the same.

It works like this. Fifty to seventy participants are divided into three groups and given colour-coded team names like Orangevale, Redvale, and Bluevale. They are told the City Game is a competitive team-building activity. Their goal is to develop the best model city using nothing more than paper, tape, scissors, and their imagination. This, of course, is not the true learning objective of the game, which is not revealed.

With everyone in the same large room, masking tape marks physical boundaries, giving each team just enough room to stand in a circle. In this tight space, team members have to collaborate to design and develop their ideal model community. Winners and losers are announced at the end of the game.

To ensure protocol is followed, peer facilitators are given roles. There is the Mayor's Office, which has to approve all plans and budgets, and decide who the winner of the competition is. A number of people are in the role of police, to ensure that the rules are followed. The teams are given ninety minutes to complete the task. As the Game Director, I introduce the game and help it run smoothly.

What participants are not told is that the game is completely rigged. It is predetermined which community will do well and which will not. In this case, team Red—which also has fewer people than average—will receive the most support. Orange—which has the most people—will encounter the most obstacles, and Blue will fall somewhere in the middle both in size and support.

Red will receive approval on the first plan and budget they submit, regardless of what it is, and begin building their city within the first ten to fifteen minutes. The plan Orange submits will be sent back several times, so that they will be unable to begin building for about thirty minutes. Blue will be somewhat delayed in their plan, but not as much as Orange.

The police will start harassing the Orange team early, from asking them to make sure they aren't stepping on the tape boundary to taking one or two people to the designated jail. In jail the "rule-breakers" will be forced to undergo punishments like doing push-ups, singing songs, or reciting goofy poetic apologies for a few minutes. It's mostly in jest, but after a while, it starts to grate on the nerves of those who, like Marco, are regularly targeted.

On the other end of the spectrum, the Red team gets accolades for whatever they do, with easy access to resources (extra tape, markers, and so on) and direct visits from the Mayor's Office. Team Blue experiences some setbacks to their plans, but not as many as the targeted group.

As Game Director, I act in a devious manner that maximizes the dynamics of privilege and marginalization. I am duplicitous in what I say and do, especially to the victimized team, Orange. I act concerned when I hear charges of "police brutality" and "unfairness," promising to do something to follow up with the Mayor's Office and police. But since the conspiracy is predetermined, there is no real improvement. To make a show of authenticity, every once in a while I will rebuke a police officer or get someone out of jail.

The heat gets turned up about halfway through the game, with the victimized Orange community experiencing everything from natural disasters to drug raids and rezoning, which reduces the size of their already overcrowded space. So even when this large group is just starting to get somewhere, some incident sets them back.

The result by the end of the time period is always the same. The privileged group, Red, has a very well organized town that looks fabulous, usually filled with business districts and residential areas, hospitals, schools, and community centres, airports, amusement parks, and even beaches. The middle group, Blue, has something decent looking, but not nearly as sophisticated as the Red town. And the group targeted for poor treatment, Orange, is usually sitting in a heap of crumpled papers, with some members running amok and screaming for revolution.

Observers usually find it difficult to stay quiet as they watch the crazy antics and unfolding chaos. Everything is so obvious, it's hard not to laugh out loud.

So what's the point? What can this exercise possibly teach us about privilege and power, when it's so grossly manipulated?

Although what's happening is obvious to observers, it isn't to participants. Most of the participants don't realize what's going on. And *that's* the essential lesson.

Recall, they were told this was a competition. So they are focused on the purpose of the game: to build a model city (distracted by their own lives, as we all are). It's after the City Game is over, during the debriefing session, that the true learning happens.

All of us co-conspirators remain in role, even when the bell indicating the end of the game sounds. With each group seated around their model town, the Mayor's Office proclaims who came in first, second, and third, with applause and cheering.

To spice things up for the debrief, one team at a time is invited to walk around to look at the other groups' efforts. This amps up the emotional wattage in the room. The first-place team feels pride and success, showing off their fabulous city. In contrast, the third-place team, with their tattered shantytown, experiences embarrassment, shame, and even anger.

After the groups have seen each other's cities, I ask each team a question: "What were the factors in your success or failure?" It's the contrasting reflections between the top and bottom teams that are most interesting.

The first-place team almost always says the same things. Their success was due to creating a plan, dividing up the tasks between their members, and working collaboratively to build their winning creation. They are genuinely proud of their accomplishments. And, as a group, they almost never have a sense that they were given any advantages by the Mayor's Office or police. They generally believe they got the top prize because of their hard work and merit. Remarkably, they rarely notice anything else happening in the room, in spite of the chaos impacting the persecuted team.

The members of the last-place team, Orange, usually offer a different perspective. Many tend to feel that they were unfairly targeted and regularly harassed by the police for small infractions. They identify the drug busts and natural disaster that affected their community, wiping out most of what they had managed to build. It's also common for members of the group to say that they, themselves, were to blame—that they didn't work well together, they had poor leadership, or that they had some disruptive team members.

And then the reveal happens.

We drop our masks and tell them the game was fixed. Again, the results are predictable. The group targeted for poor treatment is jubilant—*we knew it!*—while the privileged group is crestfallen and often silent. The ensuing conversation is rich. Together we reflect on how this game relates to real life, making the links to both privilege and marginalization.

Having run this activity so many times, I've learned some important transferable insights. I'll highlight three. First, regardless of who we are—our identities—it's hard to see privilege. Even during an experiential activity as overtly manipulated as the City Game, it's a blind spot for those who receive preferential positive treatment. The reality is the same for all of us because we don't *feel* our privilege when we have it, even though it may seem obvious from an external perspective.

Second, when we are in the privileged group, we are focused on our own hard work and challenges. So it's difficult to see how the system functions to reward our efforts while holding back those of others based on such flimsy factors as social identity. (Recall the resumé studies demonstrating pro-white name bias. How many people with white-sounding names would be aware of this significant advantage in the workplace?)

Finally, during the City Game, we are always conscious to create integrated groups. We mix people who, in real life, come from privileged and marginalized backgrounds based on factors such as race, gender, or class. Nonetheless, the results are consistent; the actual lived experience of the participants factors little in the process. If we are placed in the group targeted for oppression, it's common to feel negative, reactive, and helpless.

If treated as privileged, we are engaged and successful. We are invested in the game and its outcomes. Even participants who are disruptive or oppositional during the leadership program often settle down and focus when they are placed in the privileged group.

So what factors are at play here? How can we understand this last dimension of Deep Diversity—power? How does power create dominant and non-dominant groups in society, groups that, as a result of privilege or marginalization, can face very different realities and have strikingly different needs?

The previous three components of this framework—emotions, bias, and tribes—emphasize how we are similar. Not so for power. Power—the distribution of socio-economic and political power—is what entrenches differences between groups, amplifying feelings of "us" and "them." And this kind of all-pervasive power is the key ingredient that escalates individual acts of discrimination into systemic problems such as racism or sexism.

The framework provided by social dominance theory will help illustrate how the elements at play in the City Game—privilege and power— are magnified across society.

Systemic Discrimination

Psychologists Jim Sidanius of Harvard University and Felicia Pratto of the University of Connecticut conducted studies and synthesized research from countries around the globe. They uncovered something very important about human cultures and, perhaps, our intrinsic nature. Social hierarchies exist in all nations, creating inequality and serving as the source of most forms of intergroup conflict.[1]

They drew on research from countries including the United States, Canada, Mexico, Germany, Netherlands, Sweden, Israel, Palestine, Kenya, South Africa, Russia, India, China, Taiwan, Japan, Australia, and New Zealand. Regardless of where we live, privilege and marginalization seem to be an integral part of the human experience.

Sidanius and Pratto's framework, called social dominance theory, states that a dominant group exists in each society. The group receives privilege based on a relatively arbitrary value such as race, ethnicity, clan, or caste due to historical, economic, and political reasons specific to that context. There is no innate or natural reason for such dominance to occur—no one social group is more capable or deserving than another. But it happens. It's always happened. It seems to be something in our human nature.

Usually a group at the top of the power pyramid is granted automatic privilege—unearned higher status based simply on their group identity. All other groups—usually defined by a "minority" status—exist in a hierarchical order below and experience a greater or lesser degree of marginalization.

Sidanius and Pratto's research shows that social dominance is based on variables that are specific to each context and consistent over time. They argue, for example, that in Europe—a place known for castles, kings, and commoners—class is the historically dominant force.[2] Although race plays a significant part, it's a lesser one. In contrast, in the United States and Canada, race is the most consistent factor. Class plays an important but secondary role.

The two researchers have identified a variety of ways in which hierarchies are supported in society, including the following:

- individual acts of discrimination
- institutional discrimination
- psychological distortions
- self-destructive behaviours
- cultural myths

Using these five factors as a basic frame, let's look at the issues of power, privilege, and marginalization relating to race.

Individual Discrimination

Prejudice, in Latin, means "to judge in advance." It is often described as a preconceived idea or belief about individuals and groups that may or may not be based on reason or reality.[3] If prejudice is the belief, discrimination is the related action. And it is the small and large daily acts of discrimination, both conscious and unconscious, building up over days, years, and generations, that support and maintain a power imbalance between dominant and non-dominant groups.[4]

We can think of many individual or private acts of discrimination. A landlord won't rent out an apartment because of the applicant's race. A police officer stops more black drivers than white. The manager of a grocery store hires only women as cashiers. Educators and employers have lower expectations of people with disabilities. And all of us tend to make less eye contact with out-group members.

Institutional Discrimination

From 2005 to 2008, I worked on an intercultural dialogue project in Netherlands. I was the house guest of a judge in that country, Hanneke. We discussed at length how unconscious racial bias might impact their criminal justice system. It might help explain the overrepresentation in the system of Moroccan, Turkish, and Caribbean youth, groups that were at the bottom of the social hierarchy. This was a relatively new concept for her, and our conversations weren't easy. During one discussion, however, Hanneke shared an insight that had deepened for her since my last visit to the country:

> When I look into the eyes of a Moroccan youth whose case I'm hearing, I don't really see anything. But this is different than when I look into the eyes of a [white] Dutch child standing in my court, as I see something behind it, something familiar. I feel something that I don't with the Moroccan child.

I was struck by the honesty and simplicity of her insight. It cut to the heart of the issue. *It's easier to have compassion and understanding for those who are most like ourselves.* As a judge, Hanneke was becoming aware that her decisions were not as "objective" as she once believed. Fairness was threatened because she experienced more feelings for those of her own tribe. Until our conversations, she had never really considered implicit bias. Nor had she been motivated to catch herself in the act, so it had remained in her uncon-scious. If a majority of a country's judges are white, like my friend, and have not considered implicit bias, what might the impact be across the entire criminal justice system?

This is how discrimination is institutionalized and becomes systemic. Leaders hold positional power and make choices that are more favour-able towards members of their own tribe—in-group bias—usually with-out awareness that their choices might be prejudiced. And extra help or concern for our in-group members is what researchers Mahzarin Banaji and Anthony Greenwald suggest is a greater problem today than hurting people from out-groups.[5]

For example, a 2012 survey conducted by *The Globe and Mail*, one of Canada's national newspapers, revealed that in the previous few years, 98 of the 100 judges appointed by the Canadian government were white.[6] This situation was exacerbated by a selection process that had no transparency or clear criteria, infuriating groups that represented racialized and Aborig-inal lawyers. They claimed their members were regularly passed over for such appointments, in spite of outstanding qualifications.[7]

Institutional discrimination can be identified by whether, over time, organizational decisions result in a disproportionate allocation of social, political, and economic wealth and benefit to certain groups over others, whether that occurs consciously or unconsciously.[8] We have to ask, are all social groups treated fairly by institutional decisions and processes? The answer is an unequivocal no.

The appointment of judges is one small piece of evidence. Mountains of data from decades of research demonstrate that dominant groups benefit more from many policies and practices than non-dominant groups do. The Sidanius and Pratto research shows that this is a global phenomenon that is evident in any nation in which it has been seriously studied.[9]

In case you are unfamiliar with this body of research, the sidebars on Income and Employment Discrimination, Unequal Treatment in Health Care, and Systemic Bias in the Criminal Justice System briefly outline some trends in employment, health care, and the justice system. This evidence illustrates consistent patterns of privilege and marginalization.

INCOME AND EMPLOYMENT DISCRIMINATION

In many societies, employment, especially full-time, is considered a measure of adulthood. Having a stable job allows us to pay taxes and contribute to the welfare of our local and national communities. By spending money earned from stable employment on goods and services, we support one another and our economy. So having a well-paying, regular job is a big deal.

A 2011 study by Sheila Block and Grace-Edward Galabuzi analyzed census data and confirmed that Canada's labour market is still "colour-coded." Racialized workers are at a significant disadvantage compared to their white colleagues. Significant trends indicate that the work racial minorities attain is more likely to be insecure, temporary, and low paying. For example, racialized Canadian men earn only 81 per cent of what their white male peers earn: $48,631 compared to $60,044, respectively (for full-time, full-year employment). Women earn less than men overall, with racialized women at the bottom of the income scale, earning only 63.4 per cent of their white, male counterparts' pay.

This in spite of the fact that racialized people have higher rates of education—including university degrees—than white Canadians do. The pattern of income disparity is not specific to new immigrants but continues through the second and third generations; members of racial minorities who were born, raised, and educated in Canada still significantly lag behind their white peers (Block and Galabuzi, 12). By the third generation, the gap narrows more for women than men.

Employment and income have an additional intergenerational component. According to the U.S. Census Bureau, the median net wealth of white households in the United States in 2011 was $89,537. This figure was 12 to 14 times larger than that of their African-American and Latino-American counterparts, who had a net wealth of $6,314 and $7,683, respectively, increasing the gap from the early 1990s. This has a long-term impact, as wealth (and poverty) is usually transferred from one generation to the next. Although the financial status of parents doesn't guarantee outcomes for the children, it is a significant factor. Employment and income, therefore, are key to maintaining the existing social hierarchy and relationships of power between racial groups.

Sources:

Sheila Block and Grace-Edward Galabuzi, *Canada's Colour Coded Labour Market: The Gap for Racialized Workers* (Canadian Centre for Policy Alternatives and The Wellesley Centre, 2011), www.policyalternatives.ca.

U.S. Census Bureau, *Survey of Income and Program Participation, 2008 Panel, Wave 10*, www.census.gov/people/wealth, March 21, 2013 (US Median Value of Assets for Households, by Type of Asset Owned and Selected Characteristics: 2011).

UNEQUAL TREATMENT IN HEALTH CARE

Bias plays a significant role in health outcomes for racialized people. A 2002 study by the Institute of Medicine in the United States found overwhelming evidence that African-Americans, people of Hispanic origin, and Native Americans were much less likely to receive coronary artery angioplasty or bypass surgery, advanced cancer treatment, renal transplantation, or surgery for lung cancer (Geiger). This was in comparison to white patients of similar socio-economic and health backgrounds (age, insurance, education, and severity of disease). The report found that even basic elements of clinical care, ranging from physical examinations to history taking and lab tests, were worse for racial minorities.

Race, today, is considered a social determinant of health, meaning that racism significantly increases our chances of sickness (Mikkonen and Raphael). Although the mechanisms are complex, recall the role implicit bias played in decisions made by emergency room physicians. It's also clear that the psychological distress of discrimination creates health problems that range from migraines and backaches to impacts on cardiovascular and immune systems (high blood pressure, diabetes, and heart attacks) (Lovell).

In the United States, white people have a seven-year-longer life expectancy than their black counterparts and suffer significantly lower rates of a variety of diseases—breast cancer, heart disease, prostate cancer, as well as health conditions such as nervous and mental disorders (Sidanius and Pratto, 192).

If systemic bias keeps non-dominant groups in society in poorer health than dominant groups, the relative power dynamic between groups is maintained. If your people are generally sicker than the dominant group, it's one additional challenge to getting ahead in life.

Sources:

Jack Geiger, "Racial Stereotyping and Medicine: The Need for Cultural Competence," *Canadian Medical Association Journal* 164,12 (June 2001), 1699–1700.

Alexander Lovell, *Racism, Poverty and Inner City Health: Current Knowledge and Practices* (Hamilton Urban Core Community Health Centre, 2008), www.hucchc.com.

J. Mikkonen and D. Raphael, *Social Determinants of Health: The Canadian Facts* (Toronto: York University School of Health Policy and Management, 2010).

Jim Sidanius and Felicia Pratto, *Social Dominance: An Intergroup Theory of Hierarchy and Oppression* (New York: Cambridge University Press, 1999).

SYSTEMIC BIAS IN THE CRIMINAL JUSTICE SYSTEM

In Canada alone, more than fifteen reports since the 1970s on the relationship between the police and minority groups have clearly demonstrated the existence of racial profiling (Brown). It took until 2005, however, for the first police department in the country—from the small city of Kingston, Ontario—to openly conduct a data collection project. They were shocked to learn that the results, indeed, demonstrated that both Aboriginals and blacks were more likely to be stopped than their white counterparts ("Police Stop More Blacks"). By 2009, Toronto Police Chief Bill Blair also admitted that racial profiling was a problem in policing (Doolittle). Most other law enforcement agencies in both Canada and the United States, however, are still reluctant (or outright resistant) to admitting that racial profiling is a systemic problem, insisting instead that there are a "few bad apples."

Who is enforcing, and who is convicted of breaking, the laws? Here are some stats about police demographics:

- As of 2012, even the most diverse police force in Canada was highly unrepresentative of the community it serves. Less than 25 per cent of Toronto Police Service employees were racial minorities or Aboriginal, while more than 75 per cent were white. This in a city where almost 50 per cent of the population is non-white (Diversity Report). (Bias-free outreach and recruitment practices, however, are improving outcomes. Among new people hired in 2012, 58 per cent where white, 37 per cent racialized, and 5 per cent Aboriginal [Diversity Institute].)
- Journalists Jeremy Ashkenas and Haeyoun Park's race analysis of U.S. police departments in major cities in 2014 found similar results.
  - Only 25 per cent of officers were members of racial or ethnic minorities, according to the Bureau of Justice statistics. White officers were overrepresented in almost all of the communities they serve.
  - In New York City, 33 per cent of the population compared to 55 per cent of the officers identified as white.
  - In Los Angeles, only 29 per cent of the population was white; almost 70 per cent identified as black, Latino, or Asian. Yet 40 per cent of the police officers identified as white.
  - In Houston, it's even starker. White officers made up 52 per cent of the police force, yet whites were only 26 per cent the population.

Prison demographics are significantly influenced by race as well:

- Although African-Americans made up 13 per cent of the total U.S. population in 2010, they made up 40 per cent of the prison population and were imprisoned at five times the rates of whites nationally (Sekala).

- In Canada, according to 2011 statistics, Aboriginal people are about 4.5 per cent of the population, yet make up over 19 per cent of the federal offender population. Similarly, black people are 3 per cent of the population but almost 9 per cent of prisoners. White people, at 80 per cent of the general population, account for less than 63 per cent of federal inmates (Sapers).

- U.S. studies have shown that when the victims of murder or sexual assault were white and the accused black, the punishment was more severe than if the victim and accused were both black or both white, or if the victims were black and the accused were white (Sidanius and Pratto, 215).

The research unequivocally shows that non-dominant group members— whether they are of Moroccan ancestry in Netherlands, of Korean roots in Japan, of Arab background in Israel, or the Aborigines of Australia—are discriminated against in all stages of the criminal justice process. This applies from the likelihood of arrest and severity of charges filed, right through to higher rates of convictions and harsher sentences and punishment (Sidanius and Pratto, 202–217).

Sidanius and Pratto conclude that criminal justice systems around the world are heavily skewed, both consciously and unconsciously, to protect the interests of dominant group members. It may be difficult to accept that the criminal justice system serves as a de facto mechanism to keep groups "in their place" and maintain the status quo. But when we view society through the patterns that emerge across millions of people, that conclusion is difficult to deny.

Sources:

Jeremy Ashkenas and Haeyoun Park, "The Race Gap in America's Police Departments," *The New York Times*, www.nytimes.com, Sept. 4, 2014.

Maureen J. Brown, *We Are Not Alone: Police Racial Profiling in Canada, the United States, and the United Kingdom* (Toronto: African Canadian Community Coalition on Racial Profiling, 2004), 9.

Diversity Institute, Ryerson University, "Evaluation of the Human Rights Project Charter, February 2014."

Diversity Report of the Toronto Police Services, 2014.

Robyn Doolittle, "Racial Bias Exists on Police Force, Chief Says," *Toronto Star*, www.thestar.com, Sept. 30, 2009.

"Police Stop More Blacks, Ont. Study Finds," CBC News, www.cbc.ca, May 26, 2015.

Howard Sapers, *Annual Report of the Office of the Correctional Investigator 2012–2013*, Office of the Correctional Investigator, www.oci-bec.gc.ca, June 28, 2013.

Leah Sekala, "Breaking Down Mass Incarceration in the 2010 Census: State-by-State Incarceration Rates by Race/Ethnicity," Prison Policy Initiative, www.prisonpolicy.org, May 28, 2014.

Sidanius and Pratto, *Social Dominance*.

No Need for a Conspiracy

In the context of egalitarian countries like Canada and the United States, institutional discrimination exists without any undercurrents of conspiracy. Unlike in the past, no shadowy cabal of overt racists attempts to keep racialized and Aboriginal people down—there doesn't need to be one. The unconscious drive to favour those most like us, our in-group bias, is enough. All that's required is for a majority of leaders to be from the same in-group. Unconscious bias that privileges that tribe will flow through the system, like water running downhill.

We can do this without realizing it and in spite of our explicitly stated values about equality and democracy. The social hierarchy is maintained through individual leaders making decisions, enacting or following rules and procedures, and acting across corporate, public, and not-for-profit institutions, including the courts, police, media, health care services, schools, banks and big business, and governmental as well as religious organizations.

Of course this does not mean that, due to their identity, 100 per cent of the people are affected by privilege (or marginalization) 100 per cent of the time. But unfair treatment based on who we are happens with enough consistency that it is a significant social problem. This fosters distrust among non-dominant group members and holds back the lives of many hardworking individuals and communities. Further, such bias and favouritism function in society to create giant cultural and social blind spots.

Psychological Distortions

Part of my personal story involves desiring to be white when I was growing up, to the point that I avoided kids of my own South Asian ethnicity. Called *internalized racism*—the incorrect belief that our group (its norms, culture, and people) is inferior—this is one of the potential psychological impacts of power on non-dominant group members.

In the City Game, some participants in the group targeted for unfair treatment spoke about this feeling—that their team did not have enough leadership or teamwork, that their situation was somehow their fault. The seeds for self-doubt and insecurity were taking root, even within a simple ninety-minute activity.

We've known about this effect for a long time.

A famous 1947 U.S. study that demonstrated a majority of black children preferred to play with white rather than black dolls. Researchers found that the black children felt that the white doll was not only more attractive, with nicer skin colour, but was also "good." The black doll, in contrast, was considered ugly and "bad." Interestingly, the white doll was preferred even more by black kids in integrated schools in the north than by their peers in segregated schools in the south.[10]

When I described this study to education leaders during a 2012 conference, a diversity officer from a school district in southwest Ontario shared how accurate those results still are today. As a standard practice, the administration provides dolls of different races to kindergarten classes. They consistently find that white dolls need to be replaced regularly—indicating high use—whereas dolls of colour are preferred less for play by kids of all backgrounds, including in schools with large populations of racialized students.

Although many may argue that all groups are equally *ethnocentric*—that we prefer those from our own in-group—that is only partly true. Power, our group's status, is a major factor in how we view and value our own group compared to other groups.

Internalized dominance—the incorrect belief, conscious or unconscious, by dominant group members that their group's values, norms, culture, and people are superior—is the story from the other side of the coin. For whites, the dominant racial group, a large body of research demonstrates greater levels of ethnocentrism and in-group bias than among those who are non-dominant. For example, in North America, white people tend to show a greater average pro-white bias than blacks show pro-black bias or those of Asian ethnicity show a pro-Asian bias.[11]

Although many studies indicate that pro-black bias, for example, has increased within the black community over the decades, that has mostly occurred at the *explicit* level (what people say about themselves).[12] Although this is important, Implicit Association Tests indicate that at least 50 per cent of black Americans still have an unconscious anti-black, pro-white bias.[13] And as has been demonstrated, our implicit bias is a more accurate predictor of our behaviour and choices than what we explicitly say about ourselves.

In fact, in many cases around the world, there is a tendency for low-status group members to think less of themselves than of high-status group members. This has been found among the Maori of New Zealand, Ethiopian Jews in Israel, and black children in the Caribbean, to name just a few examples.[14]

Self-Destructive Behaviours

We also need to examine how our own choices contribute to problems of marginalization. I offer this next part of Sidanius and Pratto's framework with care and some trepidation. It's a part of the picture, but one that can easily be turned into blaming the victim. With this caution in mind, we can probably all recall choices that we or others have made that hindered rather than helped the situation.

I was a fairly new teacher when the words of thirteen-year-old Faith stunned me: "Like my mom, I'll probably be on welfare." This mixed-race child suddenly landed in my classroom one day in the spring, with a hard-edged attitude and unpredictable behaviour. Some mornings, her face was open and clear and she would really engage in learning like any other student. Other days, Faith would turn up mid-morning, pale-faced like she'd been up all night, and bark at anyone who crossed her path, including me. Sometimes she didn't show up at all.

When I collected homework, she would make an excuse to go to the bathroom or get into a fight with one of her classmates. Over time, I discovered that she would rather do this than feel incompetent or embarrassed in front of her peers. During health class, her questions and answers suggested she knew a bit too much about sex for someone her age. Early in my teaching career, I was learning from Faith about *self-sabotage*—the use of unhelpful thoughts and actions to cope with difficult feelings and existing problems.[15] I was never certain whether her behaviours were the result of poverty, racism, violence at home, or something else. The classroom structure and my teacher training didn't offer many tools to help. The only thing clear to me was that her self-harming behaviours outweighed her self-helping strategies.

After twenty years of work on issues of education and learning, it's now also clear to me that her negative actions were not innate. A child in her early teens is hardly to blame for the circumstances of her life—she had no choice in the family or context that she was born into. When we feel powerless or helpless, or when essential needs in our life are not met, we lash outwards or inwards—and often both. In a home or community in which poverty, racism, and violence intersect, opportunities to fall into despair, negativity, and self-destruction are plentiful.

This does not imply that life outcomes are predestined for a child like Faith. Our paths separated after she graduated, so I don't know the arc of Faith's story. If her life bent towards the statistics, then her chances were not great. But there are individuals in similar situations who get past self-destructive behaviours when they have key supports in place.

Students like Javier Espinoza. Now a public speaker, he describes learning from his courageous mother, who took her four kids and fled her abusive husband and worked hard to make ends meet, taking menial, exploitive jobs.[16] He also credits the shelter his family stayed in and the role of a mentor who helped him question where he was going with his life and how he might help others who were in similar situations.

Without such supports, self-sabotaging behaviours reinforce the institutional trends that keep many non-dominant group members on society's margins from achieving their potential. Javier, against statistical probability, attended university. Today, he gives back to his community by working in the field of domestic violence.

As Javier's story demonstrates, given the right circumstances, we can make individual decisions to help ourselves. This is possible even in situations where cultural or societal pressure pushes us to make self-destructive, marginalizing decisions.

In the context of education, for example, Sidanius and Pratto show that some marginalized youth develop oppositional attitudes towards teachers and the education system in general. Like Marco experienced in the City Game, negative encounters with authority figures can lead to disruptive behaviour and little interest in playing by "the rules of the game." Sidanius and Pratto point to studies focused on racialized youth from inner city contexts, which indicated that achieving academic success was sometimes stigmatized as "acting white." Teachers and school administrators were distrusted, due to perceived and real discriminatory practices. These marginalized youth considered rejection of academic success to be an act of resistance or defiance to a system of oppressive education.[17]

Laurence Steinberg's longitudinal study tracked more than 20,000 U.S. high school students from the mid-1980s, following them over a ten-year period. This research found that inferior academic performance of Latinos and blacks could be attributed to their cutting class more often, doing less homework, being less focused on their school, and being less engaged in academic achievement.[18] Again, the results are not limited to the United States. This dynamic between students from dominant and non-dominant groups is repeated across the globe, including in Canada, Australia, Bangladesh, Belgium, Czechoslovakia, Denmark, England, France, Germany, Kenya, Pakistan, Sri Lanka, and Sweden.

Sidanius and Pratto also suggest that academic success is influenced by whether youth believed educational achievement was linked to factors within their own control, such hard work and effort.[19] In contrast, the more students felt success was determined by uncontrolled influences, such as native intelligence or early school experiences, the less well they did. Most curious about this finding was that the longer an immigrant group was in the United States, the more they began to believe factors were outside their control and the less well they did academically. Although this finding was more true for some groups (blacks, Latinos) than others (Asians, whites), it suggests something important. The longer we experience marginalization, the more psychologically vulnerable we become to negative beliefs about what we are capable of.

Beyond education, evidence suggests that self-debilitating behaviours are broader among non-dominant group members than among their dominant counterparts.[20] Such behaviours include higher drug abuse, higher rates of child and spousal abuse, and a greater tendency to use extreme violence to resolve disputes. The research suggests these behaviours come from feelings of inferiority, self-loathing, and inner-directed aggression.

Recall, from chapter 2, the overlap between social and neural pain in the brain. Even a few minutes of exclusion during an insignificant online game can result in feelings of low self-esteem and lack of control. Consider what might happen if we consistently experience being left out and stigmatized, the effect magnified over years, decades, or generations.

Self-destructive behaviours are thus directly linked and nurtured by institutional discrimination. For example, Alejandra was a poor student of Mexican immigrants who scored high marks from a rigorous academic program in Santa Barbara, California. Nonetheless, in her graduating year of 2008, her guidance counsellor steered her towards a community college instead of encouraging her to pursue her dream of a four-year university degree.[21] In 2007, a human rights complaint against the Province of Ontario eliminated "zero tolerance" policies for bad behaviour in schools because, for similar infractions, racialized students were suspended and expelled at much higher rates than their white counterparts.[22]

If it looks like members of my tribe are consistently being mistreated in and by the "system"—that we're on the wrong side of statistical probability—helplessness and hopelessness can set in. These feelings can give many self-destructive behaviours logical merit. What would possibly make me think I will be the one to defy the odds?

Low expectations, unfair discipline, and misrepresentation of culture are just a few of the ways that institutional discrimination can contribute to self-destructive behaviours. The result is Faiths who expect a future on welfare, Alejandras with college rather than university degrees, and inner city, racialized youth cutting classes and dropping out without high school diplomas because they believe educational success is outside their control. In other words, negative psychological impact on non-dominant groups is one more factor bolstering the hierarchical power position of dominant groups.

Consensual Cultural Myths

Deborah Barndt was the university professor who taught me Antonio Gramsci's concept of *hegemony*. She explained that hegemony is power wielded through ideology. Standing at the front of the class, she wiggled the fingers of one hand, pointing down like a puppeteer manipulating dolls on a string. "It's coercion from above," she said, "combined with consent from below." The fingers of her other hand pointed upwards, wriggling like little dancing worms in response to the invisible strings from her top hand.

Sidanius and Pratto, summarizing the work of Gramsci and others, describe societies having enduring cultural myths that are believed by large numbers of people from both dominant and non-dominant groups.[23] The consensual nature of cultural myths is another factor that reinforces hierarchical relationships between groups.

For example, in the United States, one of the oldest myths is the so-called American dream—that socio-economic and political success is available to anyone who works hard. The flip side is equally enduring: if you

THE PROTESTANT ETHIC AND MERITOCRACY

Much has been written on the synergy between capitalism and the Protestant work ethic in European and North American society. Protestantism—and particularly Puritanism, which originated out of the Church of England—was brought by early colonists to Canada and the United States. These values shaped the moral and economic backgrounds of the two countries. While the countries have developed their own histories and political landscape, Protestant values remain culturally significant.

The Protestant work ethic emphasizes hard work, sacrifice, frugality, and self-discipline as virtuous. Calvinism, a branch of Protestant theology, suggests that wealth accumulation is a show of one's favoured standing within the religion. To accumulate wealth is to show that one is predestined to the fortunes of heaven. Conversely, poverty and unemployment can be inferred to show a disfavour with God.

The cultural influence of Calvinist doctrine moulds modern conservative beliefs of the primacy of the "individual" to succeed or fail in a marketplace that is presumed to be fair. In North American society, individuals are presumed to succeed through hard work. Individuals fail as a result of "laziness." People are considered either deserving or undeserving. This template of deserved success and failure is often applied to cultures and races.

Applying the concepts of the work ethic and of deserving and undeserving people, racial hierarchies can form where some groups are seen as more capable and deserving than others. Many people hold biases that consider Asians to be "hard-working" and black people or Native people to be "lazy and entitled." A political perspective that racializes redistributive policies (welfare) or that opposes corrective policies (affirmative or equity hiring) assumes that the system is inherently fair and that people are either poor, middle class, or rich as a result of their individual effort.

Sources:

Christopher D. DeSante, "Working Twice as Hard to Get Half as Far: Race, Work Ethic, and America's Deserving Poor," *American Journal of Political Science* 57,2 (April 2013), 342–56.

George Rawlyk, "Religion in Canada: A Historical Overview," *Annals of the American Academy of Political and Social Science* 538, Being and Becoming Canada (March 1995), 131-42.

Max Weber, *The Protestant Ethic and the Spirit of Capitalism* (Taylor & Francis e-Library, 2005).

don't achieve social or economic success, you didn't work hard enough. This belief in *meritocracy*—that anyone can make it if they put in the work—has deep Protestant roots that lead back to the founding of the nation. This ethic is also strong in Canada and similarly tied to the nation's origin (see sidebar: The Protestant Ethic and Meritocracy).

An extension to the American dream myth is the belief that racial minorities have just as good a chance as whites do to get jobs, education, and housing. Gallop polls conducted in 1997, 2007, and 2009 confirmed that a majority of the U.S. population believe this to be true.[24] A wide majority of whites and about half of blacks believed there was equal opportunity. Sidanius and Pratto point out that the differences in belief are not as remarkable as the similarities. This belief persists in spite of clear evidence, and our own everyday experiences, that institutional discrimination greatly hinders racialized people generally and black people specifically. People of colour are disadvantaged in multiple areas of their lives, including health care, employment, education, and legal justice. Yet the belief in the American dream holds strong, with half of the racialized population believing in equal opportunity. That's the power of a cultural myth.

And the American dream *is* true for many people, including, spectacularly, President Barack Obama. He overcame humble roots, including both racial and economic barriers, to win the most powerful elected position on the planet. His story and those of other successful people seem to have important psychological impacts on the rest of us.

For one, we tend to remember and be affected by stories of individuals rather than the plight of faceless millions.[25] Second, Obama, as a positive exemplar, helps justify—both consciously and unconsciously—a sense that the system is inherently fair because "he made it." The implicit suggestion is that racialized people are successful (or not) because of their own strengths or weaknesses. This perspective takes attention away from systemic issues such as racism or poverty. It's easier to remember the individuals who defy statistical odds.

Obama and His Preacher

In 2008, two race-related events caught my attention. Although they were separated by significant geography and context, they were linked in content.

Close to home, the school board in my city announced that it would create a black-focused school to address disproportionately high rates of failure among black students. This controversial decision had been over a decade in the making. A multilevel government task force on education had first introduced the idea. Whenever this issue was raised, heated debates about race followed.

Reacting to the decision, proponents of the school were happy and relieved that some positive steps were being taken to address a huge historical problem. If it was successful, perhaps learnings from this experiment could be transferred to regular schools? Critics of this initiative, some of whom were black, were upset. They argued that "segregation" and "reverse racism" were not going to fix the problems.

Across the border, a higher profile event was taking place. Barack Obama, prior to his historic win to become the first black president of the United States, was still competing with Hillary Clinton for the Democratic candidacy. At the same time, the church to which he belonged—Trinity United Church of Christ in Chicago—came under scrutiny due to inflammatory comments made by its longtime pastor, the Reverend Jeremiah Wright.[26]

I was flipping channels one night and stumbled across a conservative TV personality, Sean Hannity, interviewing Rev. Wright about allegations that he was running a black separatist church.[27] In the segment, Hannity quoted directly from the mission statement on the church's website, which explicitly stated:

Commitment to the Black community.
Commitment to the Black family.
Adherence to the Black work ethic . . .
Strengthening and supporting Black institutions . . .
Pledging support to Black leadership who embrace the Black value
system.

Hannity asked, What if a church with a white congregation specified a similar racial focus in its mission statement—but replaced "black" with "white"? Wouldn't that church be considered racist?

The reverend gave a complex (and somewhat confusing) response about liberation theology. Hannity pushed back and asked Wright to address the specific question about racism. The discussion devolved from that point, with both men talking over each other, at once defensive and aggressive.

Oh, brother, I thought to myself, is this what passes for an interview these days?

The TV clip, however, stayed with me. I thought Hannity had asked an important question (although I'm cynical of the motivations and sincerity. His modus operandi tends towards spectacle and polemic).

Hannity's core message was challenging: "I think as a Christian . . . you should not separate by race in this day and age." Another interviewee made the point that Trinity United's mission statement did not advocate black superiority but rather restated the principles of self-reliance and self-help—the very values conservatives like Hannity profess. But I wasn't satisfied that the original question was fully answered. It's a question that comes up frequently in racially charged contexts.

The undercurrent to Hannity's argument was that we live in a post-racial, colour-blind society. Exhibiting black pride—even under the banner of self-reliance—should be regarded as racially dangerous, like demonstrations of white pride by members of the Ku Klux Klan. Hannity's comments, the most powerful of the interview, were a hallmark of astute conservative political strategy: simple questions (and solutions) for complex problems.

Similar conversations occur about programs that seek to improve outcomes for historically disadvantaged groups, such as affirmative action (known as *employment equity* in Canada and *positive discrimination* in Europe). My impression is that a handful of people believe these programs are important and helpful initiatives, while another handful find them distasteful and discriminatory, describing them as "reverse racism." The rest fall somewhere in between these positions, with most remaining unclear about the need for such programs.

The central question can be distilled to this: *In egalitarian, democratic societies, should minority groups be treated differently and given greater licence on certain issues? Or should "they" always be held to the same standards as "everyone else"?*

The Unanswered Question

Looking at tribes through the lens of social dominance theory, we see that dominant and non-dominant groups can have experiences of living in the same society that are not only very different but very unequal. The buildup of individual and institutionalized discrimination over time combines with the belief in consensual myths, giving our tribes distinct psychological and material realities based on social identities.

Although it is hard for many of us to accept, the net consequence is a racial hierarchy that was designed by, and for, white people. White tribe members still benefit today more than their racialized and Aboriginal counterparts. (Again, this doesn't mean 100 per cent of the people are affected by their racial identity 100 per cent of the time, but it happens with enough consistency that it is a huge social problem.) Because groups do not start on an even playing field, what they need to achieve their human potential is very different.

So, should black-focused churches and schools be allowed when "white only" is not? I believe the answer is a solid "maybe."

Sometimes they are very needed. When a local institution like a church or school is created to serve a non-dominant group, and explicitly states, for example, a commitment to the "black family" or to "black businesses," it's an attempt to help blunt the material and psychological impact of systemic discrimination. Social spaces in which role models, positive stories, and institutional decisions are made with the non-dominant group explicitly in mind can improve self-esteem and normalize our identities. This is particularly the case when the non-dominant group is involved in the planning and decision making. In the context of Deep Diversity, such institutions open a space to create new habits—new neural pathways—that can reduce internalized psychological distortions about our tribe.

If I'm white—the norm in society—such seemingly small things may be taken for granted. They are part of the package of privilege. It is relatively easy to be immersed in environments where my tribe is the bulk of the population and of the decision makers. It's usually a safe assumption that my school will have people who look like me, including peers, teachers, administrators, principals, and trustees. I may be unaware that the curriculum I study is built on white, European values and history. Invisibly, neural pathways are nurtured that help me feel like my tribe is—and therefore, I am—normal, rather than a cultural outsider. The same may be true for the church or religious institution I choose to attend. This is how privilege operates in daily life.

Whiteness results in easy access to a multitude of role models and positive stories about the white in-group. They combine with an invisible, unconscious momentum that supports an individual's progress through institutions. Relatively few forces hold white people back from developing their human potential in society. That is not the case for many racialized and Aboriginal people.

The crux of the matter is that creating a space for non-dominant groups must be a *conscious* act. This explicitness is what gets some people emotionally worked up. For the dominant tribe, however, society already is designed in our favour—racial privilege, unconscious and therefore invisible, is taken for granted.

In this historical period, it is significantly different for a church, school, or organization in Canada or the United States to have a "black-focused" mandate than a "white-focused" or "white only" mandate. In the current reality, white people are the majority population and hold the bulk of decision-making positions in society. Without consciously seeking it, if I am white, I can live, work, learn, and play in many, many places across both nations, where decisions unconsciously and consciously are made to support me and my identity.

And when this reality is coupled with the trauma of North America's violent pro-white past, there is good reason to be wary of organizations explicitly wanting to be "white only." (And pro-white groups are quite different from cultural groups that celebrate their British, Irish, or Dutch ethnicities.) As the population balance changes, consciously managing shifting power structures becomes even more important. In Canada and the United States, it is generally accepted that sometime in the second half of this century, the scales will tip and whites will become a minority. If we do not learn to share power, what will our lives look like with a white minority as the dominant group? Or if we don't learn from our experiences, will the tables simply be turned, with whites becoming marginalized?

When Segregated Spaces Are Okay

If girls-only classes result in better performance in math, then why not offer the option of sex-segregated classrooms? If regional health services with a specific Aboriginal focus are more effective than mainstream medical facilities, why not offer more of them?

We've always known that one size does not fit all. That's especially the case for issues of race. Of course, I'm not talking about institutionally or state-enforced segregation, but about places where the underlying assumption is that we have a *choice* to join or not join such an intentional program or organization. There is an important positive side to optional segregated spaces.

Such environments, however, can also result in the promotion of hate rather than healing. That is why my response was a clear "maybe." If groups work to promote violence, fear, and animosity—regardless of whether the groups are socially dominant or non-dominant—then I believe they are unhealthy, unhelpful, and should be stigmatized.

HANDLING GUNS: A BLACK AND WHITE ISSUE

Several incidents demonstrate that race plays a role in who can display guns—even toy guns—in public in the United States.

1. While in a Walmart in Ohio in August 2014, John Crawford made the tragic mistake of picking up an air rifle from a shelf—a regular store item—while he casually talked on his cell phone. He is captured on store video minding his own business and occupied with his call in an empty store aisle with no other customers around. The toy gun is pointed down, the barrel resting on his foot, when two police officers charge in, shooting and killing him. Crawford was black.

2. In a Walmart in Idaho in December 2014, two drunken men entered the store, grabbed a BB gun from the shelf, loaded it, and started shooting inside the store, threatening staff and shoppers. Four shots were fired before they fled the store and, shortly thereafter, were arrested by police "without incident." Both men were white (photos but not names were released).

3. In November 2014 in Cleveland, Ohio, twelve-year-old Tamir Rice was captured on video walking around in a small park playing with a toy gun. He points the gun around—there are no other people nearby in the frame—he walks back and forth seeming bored, he kicks snow stuck to the curb. A police car zooms into the scene and pulls up next to Tamir. An officer jumps out and shoots the child. Tamir's fourteen-year-old sister is shown in a second video rushing to her younger brother's aid following the gunfire, but is tackled by a second officer and handcuffed. Tamir and his sister were both black.

4. In late December 2014 in Chattanooga, Tennessee, a forty-three-year-old woman, Julia Shields, drove around an upscale neighbourhood dressed in body armour, shooting at random people and cars. She pointed her gun at a police officer as well as at children. Police gave chase by car and on foot. She was apprehended without incident or injury and charged with three counts of attempted first-degree murder. Shields was white.

Sources:

Kendi Anderson, "Woman Shoots Up Hixson Neighborhood," timesfreepress.com, Dec. 28, 2014.

"Cleveland Police Handcuff Tamir Rice's Sister after Shooting 12-Year-Old—Video," *The Guardian*, www.theguardian.com, Jan. 8, 2015.

Dan Kennedy, "Update: Children Witnessed Shields' Alleged Shooting Spree," WRCBtv.com (Chattanooga), Dec 27, 2014.

"North Idaho Briefs: Men Arrested after Wal-Mart BB Gun Incident," CDAPress.com, Dec. 26, 2014.

"Ohio Walmart CCTV Captures John Crawford Shooting—Video," *The Guardian*, Sept. 25, 2014.

"Tamir Rice: Police Release Video of 12-Year-Old's Fatal Shooting—Video," *The Guardian*, Nov. 26, 2014.

The issue then becomes who decides what is and isn't considered hate and violence. Again, it comes down to power. Who gets to define the problem and create the solutions? For example, if non-dominant groups are critical, outspoken, or angry about issues like racism, sexism, or poverty, they are more likely to be regarded as a threat than others. Dominant group members, doing the same thing, usually have more leeway as a result of their privilege.

For example, in 2010 in New Mexico, three hundred people from the Tea Party movement—predominantly white, conservative, and middle-aged—displayed their dislike of the U.S. federal government, symbolized by President Obama, by carrying guns at a protest.[28] In the prior year, there were several incidents involving protestors with guns at presidential events, including during a town hall meeting in New Hampshire.[29] There, a man with a loaded gun strapped to his leg carried a sign with a famous quote: "The tree of liberty must be refreshed from time to time, with the blood of patriots and tyrants." The threat of violence in these events was not only self-evident but also openly stated.

These and other similar incidents directed towards Obama garnered some coverage and reaction, but not a great deal. This makes some sense in the context of the United States. Guns are an intimate part of society, and "open carry" laws in many states allow for loaded firearms to be worn and displayed in public (including by teachers in schools).[30] It is harder to find the contextual and historical logic for these protests being considered non-racial in nature. They were, however, mostly portrayed as citizens protesting against a government they didn't choose.

Which brings us back to who decides what's an expression of hate and violence. Would the response have been different if hundreds of black people were protesting *with guns* against a white president, like George W. Bush? Would the protest be seen as more or less violent? Would it be seen through a racial lens by the media, public, or government?

The scathing public reaction to Rev. Jeremiah Wright, a controversial figure because of his criticism of U.S. national and international policies, suggests that the reaction would be different. There is no doubt Wright was outspoken, critical, and even flamboyantly aggressive in his style. But he carried no gun, nor did he suggest violence.

A group of black Americans protesting with guns would evoke a very different—likely swift and strong—reaction by both public and government officials. Scientifically, it's a strong bet. Recall the implicit bias shooter tasks, where most people will incorrectly shoot unarmed blacks while sparing armed whites.

This point was driven home in a horrifying manner in 2014 with the shooting deaths of fourteen-year-old Tamir Rice, who carried a toy gun at a park, and twenty-two-year-old John Crawford, who was in a Walmart and picked up a common store item—a kid's air rifle—while he was talking on a cell phone. White people doing similar or worse things around the same time were arrested "without incident." (See sidebar: Handling Guns for details.)

I suspect that this on-the-ground reality is part of the reason that protestors—many of them people of colour—who expressed outrage following various tragic deaths of this nature, including those of Michael Brown and Eric Garner, did not express their dissatisfaction by openly carrying weapons en masse. Their white Tea Party counterparts, though, felt entitled to do so.

The point is not about guns. It is about the reality that privilege often grants entitlement and protection that the marginalized cannot count on in the same way.

Inner Skill 5: Self-Education

The inner skill to complement an analysis of power, privilege, and marginalization is self-education. Personal effort is required to understand that whether we like it or not, or are aware of it or not, the tribes we belong to matter, especially those based on race and ethnicity. Decades of reports and information are available about systemic discrimination in both Canada and the United States. Although our personal experience is a valuable source of information, so are the patterns revealed by data that compare groups of people over time. Our experience may not reveal our blind spots. But it's possible that our experience, seen through the lens of learning and research, may offer us a glimpse of what we are not seeing.

Self-education is really shorthand for taking personal responsibility to understand what the impact of systemic discrimination means for ourselves and our communities—who's doing well, who's struggling, and why. Honouring the values of our egalitarian, democratic society requires this much from us.

However, confronting such information is not simply an intellectual exercise. It usually evokes a wide variety of internal responses and emotions. Some may be helpful (such as humility, curiosity, and motivation) and others less so (defensiveness, guilt, rage). Therefore, the previously mentioned inner skills, including self-awareness, self-regulation, and empathy, are required to navigate terrain that, at first glance, may seem very cerebral in nature.

Self-education may take a variety of forms, including the following:

- *Self-study*. Informally and on our own time, digging deeper into the issues of race and systemic discrimination, to better understand ourselves and our tribe in the context of the greater whole. A wide variety of resources on this subject is available online, in books and journals, and in mainstream and alternative news sources.
- *Learning through relationship*. Immersing ourselves in environments and activities that expose us to people of different ethno-

cultural identities to build personal connections and two-way relationships. There is no limit to where or how this happens: employee resource groups at work, events at community centres, joining sports or arts organizations, or connecting with neighbours we know less well. The online world can also help bridge physical distances, making a variety of social connections possible.

- *Formal study.* Taking courses through learning institutions such as colleges or universities.

Overwhelmed Yet?

There is more to be said about self-education and inner tools, but I have to be honest. Even as I write this chapter, I feel a little weighed down.

When I get into a structural analysis of power, two emotions usually compete for my attention. I feel empowered and, at the same time, overwhelmed.

I find the lens offered by Sidanius and Pratto empowering because it helps me see things I couldn't see before. It's helpful because my understanding of the issues deepens, fuelling my compassion and my desire to make the world a better place.

I also encounter feelings of heaviness, realizing how big the problems of racism, discrimination, and oppression are. This fuels my anger and helplessness. Part of me just wants to go back to bed.

I struggled to write this chapter on power, because it represents an inner tension between my past and present self. In the next chapter, I'll share how I spent many years using this lens on power, got depressed by the negative perspective on the world, and burned out. I'll also share tools I found that helped me tap into inner resources to maintain a hopeful yet complex outlook, so I could still wake up in the morning and take on the day.

POWER PART 2: THIS TIME IT'S PERSONAL

Limitations of a Power Analysis

AT ONE TIME, I defined myself as an anti-racist activist who was steeped in a structural power analysis similar to that presented in social dominance theory. This analysis was my predominant lens on the world. It is what I was drawn to, learned, and then taught to others. It's a powerful tool that helped me see patterns that I couldn't see before. Prior to encountering such theories of social dominance, I had not considered the distribution of resources in society, nor how decisions were made and by whom. Those who don't use this perspective may fail to take into account critical information that's necessary to enhance fairness and justice in the world.

A power analysis also helped make sense of my personal experience of feeling left out and of growing up wanting to be white. Understanding that such experiences were common to other people was a relief; what happened to me wasn't my fault. It wasn't about my deficiencies as a person, but rather, deficiencies in the culture, in institutions, and in how we've been socialized.

This perspective, however, became the exclusive lens through which I viewed the world, and it contributed to me burning out by age thirty.

Social dominance theory, anti-racism, and other theories like them examine power structurally, predominantly from a socio-economic and political perspective. As much as this is an important aspect of how power operates, it can also be a limiting framework. Given the complexities of organizations and of society as a whole, such theories of power cannot adequately capture all the nuances of our lives.

For example, in a profession that's dominated by women, such as nursing, can a man not feel and occasionally experience marginalization? Similarly, in workplaces where racial minorities are in the majority or are in positions of authority, is it not possible for a white person to struggle to find acceptance and a sense of belonging? And what about the success of non-dominant group members like President Obama who have surpassed the "sticky floor," broken through the "glass ceiling," and achieved the highest levels of success? How do we name, acknowledge, and honour such experiences?

Although the goal of a structural power analysis is to assist in liberation and emancipation, it can, like a double-edged sword, cut both ways and fuel a sense of despair. This is what happened to me, and it was a very common experience among my social justice peers.

We valued "critical thinking," but that meant offering critiques exclusively from the left of the political spectrum. *Avoid purchasing coffee, books, and clothing from large corporations. Globalization is bad. The Olympics are a waste of money and resources. All corporate media spout pro-conservative views. The problems in the world are created by straight white men.*

We were outside-the-box. Alternative. Organic. Vegetarian. We were on the side of justice and we held the moral high ground (at least from our own viewpoint). We brought our "critical perspective" everywhere we went. At dinner parties, any statement could be turned into a political moment to "educate" others. It could be a comment about the food we were eating (*toxic hormones in meats and veggies*), dishwashing soap (*phosphates poison marine life*), or critiques of mainstream politics (*all big political parties are on the right side of the spectrum*). We could critique and therefore rain on anyone's parade, including our own.

An acquaintance who also strongly held feminist anti-racist perspectives once told me she found social gatherings stressful. I was no introvert, but I could relate to what she said. I frequently had to brace myself in informal group settings, feeling an invisible pressure to somehow step in and respond to people's "ill-informed" perspectives about how the world worked. I was on guard in most contexts. I dreaded the possibility that someone might say the "wrong" thing and I'd have to "correct" them—exhausting!

I didn't realize what was happening, but pessimism and disapproval were becoming my close friends. Unaware that the dial on my negativity bias was stuck on high, I'd lost the ability to distinguish critical from cynical. After all, we were surrounded by all forms of corporate something-or-other, be they corporate media, corporate politics, or corporate agriculture. It was a bit of a bunker mentality in the trenches of social activism. We were a minority and power was not in our favour. We wanted the world to be beautiful, but our words and actions communicated that it was mostly ugly.

As it's said: what we look for, we find. When we view the world exclusively through the lens of power as defined by theories like social dominance theory, there is the danger of our perspective becoming negative and despairing. For me, life looked pretty grey. The critical lens I had adopted eventually helped me burn out. It wasn't the only factor, but it gets the nod for Best Supporting Actor in a Comedy That Is My Life.

Reflecting on this now, I've come to realize that the ways we think about things—the lenses we use—also become neurologically wired and formed into habits. When the same lens is used regularly, for example, in social activism and academics, we can almost lose choice in how we view the world. Just as privilege often begets privilege, the opposite can also happen. If we are immersed in issues of marginalization, it's hard not to see marginalization everywhere. Unless we are aware of this particular trap, we may, on the way to empowerment, inadvertently enhance our sense of victimization. They are, after all, flip sides of the same coin.

Such perspectives on power also helped neatly divide the world into specific tribes: those who "got it" and those who did not. Sub-groups included victims, perpetrators, and rescuers (us). Ironically, Us/Them was alive and kicking, being perpetuated by my social justice peers and me. We just didn't recognize it. And not surprisingly, no matter how far up on the moral high ground we are, the view is still cloudy.

Personal and Social Power: A Balanced Approach

Although I have become critical of my past orientation, I still believe that, to enhance democracy and nurture a stronger sense of inclusion, a structural analysis of power is essential. That's why the entire previous chapter was dedicated to social dominance theory. We need to uncover patterns that appear only when data is collected across large groups of people and analyzed for trends. It is important to understand how power, institutions, and structures influence our choices, interactions, and culture. Fundamentally, the goal of such a power analysis is to help alter our awareness of social norms and bring positive change at a profound scale. And that's something I firmly support.

I do take issue, though, with it being the *only* perspective on the world. We're not just cogs in a wheel. We're influenced by and influence our environments, including our families, friends, organizations, and society at large.

As my discomfort with this single perspective grew, I came across the Process Work Institute, an organization that had developed a more nuanced, balanced approach to power. Pioneered by Jungian psychologist Arnold Mindell in the 1970s, this group has been developing expertise in understanding individual and group behaviour, especially related to intergroup conflict. According to the Mindell, we have access to both *social power* and *personal power*.[1] (See sidebar: Rank and Power Model.)

We receive social power from two sources. The first is status gained from our various social identities, including race, gender, class, sexual orientation, and ability. Called *global rank*, it's the level of power we have (or are given) when we walk into a room full of strangers; it's the first impressions, both conscious and unconscious, based on what we look like and how we speak, hold, or present ourselves. We don't have a lot of control over most of these factors. They are a result of the body and circumstances we were born into.

RANK AND POWER MODEL
(ARNOLD MINDELL, PROCESS WORK INSTITUTE)

1. Social Power	**Global Rank:** Context dependent, seemingly static, associated with social norms, random (e.g., race, wealth/class, religion, gender, sexual orientation, physical ability).
	Local Rank: Context dependent, shifts rapidly, associated with local norms, values, current conditions, participants, topics (e.g., seniority or position in group, adherence to norms, popularity/insiderness, communication style).
2. Personal Power	**Psychological Rank:** Life experience, emotional fluidity, communication skills, humour, relational skills, insight into self and others.
	Spiritual Rank: Connection to larger purpose, vision, transcendent experience, knowledge of self and other, awareness of death and life.

Source:

Julie Diamond, "Deep Democracy: Creating Whole Systems Change," workshop held by Anima Leadership, Toronto, Oct. 2010, http://juliediamond.net.

The second source of social power, gained from our status in our immediate environment, may shift depending on our micro-context. Our *local rank*, for example, may be very high at work because of our executive job title. But when we go shopping for groceries, the part-time clerk has more power over decisions than we do. Such status can shift moment to moment depending on the context and the people we are around.

A key point to understand is that, at times, our local rank may temporarily trump our global rank. For example, I've been in environments in which women of colour, who may have lower global rank based on identity, possessed the highest levels of local rank—and therefore influence—within their organization. This was due to their expertise, seniority, and ability to articulate the issues. Equally I've watched white men—high global rank—have difficulty participating and speaking up. Their lower numbers and inexperience with issues in that specific micro-context held them back.

Social power is the link between Mindell's model and social dominance theory (or my early training in anti-racism), as both seek to identify the different social relationships between groups. Mindell's model acknowledges that our tribes—race, gender, class, sexual orientation, ability, and so on—are important sources of power. But they can also undermine us.

High status from our social identities (social power) is considered the most brittle type of rank. It comes largely from outside ourselves. We didn't have to do anything to gain entry, so it's an invisible privilege. In some cases, higher rank because of something like our race or sex (being white or male) may actually be disempowering. First, because we may not be aware of it, and second, because it may not make us *feel* powerful. Further, this invisible quality almost always leaves us vulnerable to making mistakes and being criticized, ridiculed, and even attacked based on our unearned privilege (and lack of awareness of it).

The real clout behind the Mindell's model comes from the next category, called personal power. This is something we all possess. Such power was drawn on by heroes of history such as Mahatma Gandhi and Dr. Martin Luther King Jr.

Arguably, these leaders had lower global rank in their contexts. Of course, each of them had some social rank to begin with; they both were middle-class, university-educated men. But in that period, race was the defining social identity. Non-white people were considered inferior and less human, and accordingly, were treated with contempt and violence. Gandhi, a lawyer by training, was still a soft-spoken brown man fighting for civil rights for his people in South Africa and India against the all-powerful British Empire. King, a church leader, was a black man living through the intensely racist pre–civil rights era United States. Both of these individuals, however, possessed inner strength and conviction, power that flowed from their psychological and spiritual qualities.

Psychological rank is status from our personal attributes—who we are and what makes us unique. These attributes include our life experiences, leadership qualities, sense of humour, self-awareness, communication skills, courage, curiosity, and community consciousness.

Personal power also comes from *spiritual rank.* This form of influence comes from the ability to make meaning of things and place ourselves within the larger framework of life. Part of this process is struggling with existential questions: *What's my purpose? Why are we here? How do I deal with life's tragedies and hardships?*

A deep knowledge of self and others and an awareness of the cycle of life and death are also markers of spiritual strength. This type of rank may or may not flow from organized religion. But usually, it is accompanied by the ability to celebrate the beauty of life while also acknowledging its brutality.

Gandhi and King both exemplified such personal power at profound levels, as did many of their peers. In the face of brutal oppression based on race—whether it was British rule in India or racial segregation in the United States—these leaders did not let their lower global rank hold them back. Their power—based on personal convictions, interpersonal skills, and deep spiritual callings—was sufficient to inspire millions to unlock their own personal power, tackle racial oppression, and create powerful social change.

But high rank in the personal power dimension is not just the domain of celebrated heroes of history. It's Javier Espinoza from California, whom we met in chapter 5. He overcame a childhood of violence to work with women and children who suffer abuse. It's the white hockey coach in the Toronto suburbs who pulled his team from the ice because of racial slurs used by the opposing team.[2] It's the passengers at a bus stand in Canada's steeltown, Hamilton, who unequivocally stood up for stranger, a Muslim man, who was the target of hateful comments by another passenger.[3]

So the good news is that we all possess personal power. The better news is that personal power can be grown and developed.

This is the most hopeful aspect of Mindell's model. We can always cultivate and increase our personal power. It can be enhanced through inner work, through developing our psychological and spiritual capacities. Personal power can be grown through any process that helps us improve our sense of who we are and how we interact with others. It helps us find purpose, meaning, and joy in our lives. Because this form of power is internal, it is more resilient than social power. And it can be applied across different contexts.

Further, changing the dynamics of social power, especially around issues of race, is a long-term project. Marginalized communities may see little immediate change to help their circumstances. Personal power, though, is more direct. Regardless of where we are in the social hierarchy, we can rely on personal power every day to make our experience of living more positive.

Developing personal power isn't anything new. We harness it whenever we attempt to make a small or big change to improve our lives. It's what support workers at a women's shelter draw on to do the work they do. Personal power is also accessed when victims of violence find ways to heal and move forward with their lives. It's at the core of peer-led leadership networks designed to help youth launch community innovation projects. Any meaningful social change project, in fact, is about em*power*ment of people—about agency rather than dependency.

In the Deep Diversity framework, personal power and the potential for change it represents can serve as a catalyst for system-wide change. There is always a dialogue, a creative tension, between recognizing the influence of institutions on the individual and of the individual on the system. The trick is holding this tension and not getting caught in the either/or polarity. This is the balance point, both emotionally and intellectually.

Blinded by Power

Developing personal power is vital for all of us, whether we belong to dominant or non-dominant racial groups. This controversy that arose at Princeton University illustrates why.

In 2014, a Princeton student named Tal Fortgang wrote an article for his school newspaper, which was republished in *Time* magazine. In his article, he said that he would never apologize for his white, male privilege. His perspective was that he got to where he was through sheer hard work and determination, suggesting that any kind of bias there might be in the system played no part in his success. His angry, unrepentant tone drew a great deal of response both from supporters and critics (see sidebar: Tal Fortgang's Article).

Briana Payton, a leader at the Princeton Black Student Union, wrote a response chastising Fortgang for his basic misunderstanding of the issue of privilege. The way she saw it, Fortgang was deluding himself to believe he had never benefited from both pro-white and pro-male biases in society. His hard work and skills weren't the only factors in his success, she argued, and meritocracy in the United States was a myth. Payton, too, sounded angry and unwavering in her position (see sidebar: Briana Payton's Response).

These polarized positions are common on the topic of race and power. They force the listener to choose one perspective or the other. But we can also use these oppositional views to deepen our understanding of what's happening.

If we can get past the either/or trap of these arguments, we may be able to recognize that both views hold some truth. In the last chapter, we looked at a great deal of evidence pointing to the systemic nature of racial bias. White people benefit from a society created with their social identity as the norm. In spite of—perhaps because of—an Ivy League background, Fortgang's privileged position misses or ignores that body of evidence. However, Payton's position also minimizes important evidence. There is no doubt that in spite of the barriers, many racialized people do actually live the American dream and achieve the highest levels of success.

One of the things I've learned is that when people are in conflict, it can be revealing to listen to the tone and energy behind the words being used. There are elements in the articles in which Fortgang and Payton mirror each other. Besides being articulate and assertive, the tonality conveys anger, defensiveness, condescension, distrust, and feelings of being misunderstood.

TAL FORTGANG'S ARTICLE: EXCERPTS

"Check your privilege," the saying goes, and I have been reprimanded by it several times this year. The phrase, handed down by my moral superiors, descends recklessly, like an Obama-sanctioned drone, and aims laser-like at my pinkish-peach complexion, my maleness, and the nerve I displayed in offering an opinion rooted in a personal *Weltanschauung*. . . .

They tell me in a command that teeters between an imposition to actually explore how I got where I am, and a reminder that I ought to feel personally apologetic because white males seem to pull most of the strings in the world. . . .

I do condemn them for diminishing everything I have personally accomplished, all the hard work I have done in my life, and for ascribing all the fruit I reap not to the seeds I sow but to some invisible patron saint of white maleness who places it out for me before I even arrive. . . .

That's the problem with calling someone out for the "privilege" which you assume has defined their narrative. You don't know what their struggles have been, what they may have gone through to be where they are. Assuming they've benefitted from "power systems" or other conspiratorial imaginary institutions denies them credit for all they've done, things of which you may not even conceive. . . .

It has been my distinct privilege that my grandparents came to America. . . . It was their privilege to come to a country that grants equal protection under the law to its citizens, that cares not about religion or race, but the content of your character. . . .

Behind every success, large or small, there is a story, and it isn't always told by sex or skin color. My appearance certainly doesn't tell the whole story, and to assume that it does and that I should apologize for it is insulting. . . . I have checked my privilege. And I apologize for nothing.

Source:

Tal Fortgang, "Why I'll Never Apologize for My White, Male Privilege," *Time*, www.time.com, May 2, 2014.

BRIANA PAYTON'S RESPONSE: EXCERPTS

While Fortgang is not responsible for white male dominance in society, he should at least recognize that this social hierarchy is not a mere coincidence, nor is it a testament to the power of hard work. Such a micro-level explanation, when applied to our country's current state, would imply that white males have by and large outworked most women and minorities in the many fields in which they dominate. . . .

Fortgang's privilege is evident in his erroneous assertion that America is "a country that grants equal protection under the law to its citizens. . . ." Such a statement fails to acknowledge that an equal protection clause in the law is not enough to effect equal treatment, nor does the law even promise that every violation will be properly handled. People of color know all too well what it means to be neglected and abused by the justice system, rather than protected by it. . . .

The real myth here is meritocracy. . . . No one is saying Fortgang did not sow seeds, but checking his privilege is just acknowledging that the ground he tilled was more fertile than the ground others tilled. They could have spent the same amount of time in the hot sun, watering these seeds, but Fortgang might still reap better results because of certain advantages. . . .

Additionally, Fortgang's ancestors' past struggle in no way negates the existence of his societal privilege today. He doesn't have to fear racial profiling or employment discrimination. The closest thing to racism that he cites is someone calling him privileged. . . .

Is that clear? You. Are. Privileged. It is OK to admit that. You will not be struck down by lightning, I promise. You will not be forced to repent for your "patron saint of white maleness" or for accepting your state of whiteness and maleness. . . .

Even as a black woman, whose race and sex has posed unique and difficult challenges, I have done a privilege check. I am privileged to come from an upper middle class family, to belong to the religious majority and to have both my parents in the home. I acknowledge this because it allows me to empathize more with others and remain humble and grateful.

Source:

Briana Payton, "Dear Privileged-at-Princeton: You. Are. Privileged. And Meritocracy Is a Myth," *Time*, www.time.com, May 6, 2014.

This peculiarity in their conflict suggests feelings of disempowerment, according to Julie Diamond, one of the co-founders of the Process Work Institute.[4] When someone belittles or minimizes the other person's perspective, they may internally be feeling low-power rather than high-power. Lashing out usually comes from a place of weakness, not strength.

According to Dr. Diamond:

> Fortgang is writing from a low-rank position, specifically at the local level of the college campus. Consider what's happening at universities right now—there is a frenzy of social justice activism. Many white kids don't have the analysis or experience because of their high [racial] status. Fortgang is coming across like a victim of the social justice warriors telling him to "check his privilege." I don't want to say he's a victim but he's speaking from a hurt, disempowered place. You can't read that situation without an alternative power analysis that also considers local rank issues specific to the college context. And local rank can often trump global rank.[5]

The oddity about privilege, as we've noted, is that it is usually invisible when we have it. It doesn't make us *feel* powerful. Ironically, Fortgang sounds like he's the casualty of an oppressive social system out to silence his voice on the basis of his gender and race. Negativity bias exacerbates his defensiveness and focus on his personal story, helping him ignore a reality that impacts racial groups on a larger scale.

Like the Red group that received preferential treatment in the City Game and couldn't see the mistreatment of their Orange peers, Fortgang is unaware of his privilege. All he can focus on is his own hard work. He seems oblivious that his odds of receiving a variety of critical life benefits, including access to jobs, better health care, and fairer treatment in the justice system are significantly better than his racialized peers'. In fact, it's easy to argue that it was because of Fortgang's privilege that his article went viral and was picked up by *Time*. Part of systemic bias is that injustice—perceived or real—faced by dominant group members is amplified, provided space politically, and taken more seriously compared to that faced by their non-dominant counterparts.

On the other side, Diamond suggests that Payton and social activists like her, who have less global rank because of race or gender, don't see how powerful they are personally. This is because of a narrow definition of power.

> When social activists like Payton are reading the riot act about privilege, they are in their power. But they don't see it clearly. They see it as just defending themselves, even though they are running circles around their opposition. They have power, insight, experience, and are very articulate. Helping them see their power is part of the solution.

Diamond argues that social activists can inadvertently become "experts on low rank." They are able to clearly see, name, and challenge how marginalization works, but may never fully acknowledge and become comfortable with their areas of high rank, where they hold the upper hand.

Activists like Payton who are focused on power imbalances related to identity (low global rank) may not see the full power they actually possess. They are able to influence, marginalize, and even silence through their skills in communication and critical racial analysis (high personal power). For many social change makers—and my personal story is a case in point— a limited definition of power makes it feel like injustice and its agents are at every corner. Coupled with our negativity bias, it becomes easy to feel disempowered and it's difficult to move beyond the victim/perpetrator, oppressed/oppressor orientation to the world.

One instrument that is frequently missing from the social activist toolkit is an awareness of the emotional and psychological impacts on people in the privileged camp. When we are challenged or criticized on our privilege, it is common to be flooded by emotions such as guilt, shame, or anger. When triggered like this, the thinking part of our brain shuts down significantly, while the reactive parts take over. In such a psychological state, it is highly unlikely for learning to take place.

The common advice by social activists to deal with privilege is to "sit with your discomfort." This is an extremely unrealistic strategy, considering people are in some variation of fight-flight-freeze. In my opinion, this directive only works for a tiny portion of the population (usually, the converted). If our goal is to help people see their privilege, an educational strategy that triggers people emotionally will be limited in its effectiveness. In fact, when one first discovers one's privilege, it takes a great deal of personal power to sit with the discomfort.

Applying Personal Power

I'd like to suggest that Fortgang's voice, although strident, echoes the views of many white people who are confused about issues of race but are otherwise well intentioned and fair-minded. For example, one participant approached me partway through a diversity training and asked: Are you going to deal with what white people can do? I'm afraid of saying the wrong thing, of making a mistake and being told I've done it wrong. She was truly distressed, vulnerable, and confused about how, as a white person, to move forward on racial inclusion.

If we are from the dominant group, personal power is necessary to help us accept that, in so many ways, our group benefits from being part of the social norm. There is systemic bias, and it plays in the dominant tribe's favour. Individuals need psychological and spiritual strength to deal with the emotions that surface with that discovery, and with the inevitable mistakes and criticism that come with possessing social privilege.

Let's be clear—the issues at stake are also about life and death. When little boys playing in parks or young men shopping in a Walmart are killed because of their skin colour while the police who shoot them are let off the hook, there is a place for not just anger but also rage, for irrationality. We *must* understand that. To deny such righteous anger would be to deny our own humanity.

Personal power is needed to listen deeply to the pain experienced by groups and individuals, rather than dismissing or minimizing their perspectives because they make us feel bad or accused. Personal power is needed to understand that we may not have created the problems, but we have responsibility to make things better. The journey of self-learning is necessary to help level the playing field for all racial groups, no matter where we are in the social hierarchy.

On the flip side is Payton's reply. In spite of the reprimanding tone, she reflects the perspectives of many non-white people who struggle with how hard it is for their racial experiences to be acknowledged by mainstream society. I'm reminded of the pain and vulnerability of living on the wrong side of privilege expressed by a black mother. She wept with frustration and anger as she said to me: Why is my son suffering the same racial taunts and humiliating schoolyard experiences that I did forty years ago? Why is this still happening?

If we are from non-dominant or minority groups, personal power is needed to not be overwhelmed at a society that is imbalanced against our tribe, and not give in to despair over the magnitude of the problems we face. Higher rank in psychological and spiritual dimensions would be necessary for Payton to recognize all the ways in which she is powerful, to see the world as a place of opportunities while also navigating the roadblocks. Personal power is needed to recognize that changing social norms is a slow but continuous process, usually beyond the scope of a single lifetime. It's also necessary to resist the temptation to dehumanize white people and turn each of them into a representative of a group, painting their whole tribe as bad or uncaring.

What would it be like if people like Fortgang and Payton could see even a little of the truth from the other perspective? If they could set their political views aside enough to be a little curious about the other person? What if they could offer their own strong perspectives, while also validating the other's view?

First of all, it would require both of them to start by seeing the person as an individual, not just as a symbol of a group. Without entirely dulling their edge, the following might be constructive suggestions for Fortgang speaking to Payton (say, over a coffee):

- I'm feeling attacked—what am I doing that makes me a target for your anger? What am I missing?
- I want to know where you're coming from, but "check your privilege" really irritates me. I've worked hard to get here; all you focus on is my skin colour and maleness. Can we begin again, from another starting point?
- You sound pissed off at me but you don't know my story and don't seem interested. Help me out here—what's that about? Am I somehow a threat to your story?

And Payton might begin speaking to Fortgang along these lines:

- Dismissing privilege as part of some "conspiratorial power systems," as you say, infuriates me and denies my lived experiences. I don't get it—why is that difficult for you to see or understand?
- Sure, you did sow seeds. So did I. But many others in our country also work hard, and water and look after their seeds, without the same results. Can we look at that, too?
- I find doing a privilege check useful to empathize with others. But you reacted strongly—why? What's different for you?

From my experience, conversations are potentially transformative when people in polarized positions are able to be empathetic to each other. There needs to be a give and take in the conversation, especially acknowledgement of other person's perspective. They might say—and genuinely feel—things like these:

- Okay, I get it. I hadn't thought of that before.
- Your experience sounds really hard . . .
- Wow—I didn't know that. I'm sorry that happened to you.

This kind of conversation shows an effort to be in relationship, to work through issues of difference.

Inner Skills 6 & 7:
Relationship Management and Conflict Skills

To be vulnerable is an act of personal power. To listen to another person's perspective and let it affect you is an act of personal power. To speak honestly and truthfully, which means standing up for yourself and your side in a conversation, is also an act of personal power.

That doesn't mean that each conversation must end up in a mushy middle ground where both sides feel they have to "compromise" important things. An authentic conversation can take us to a new understanding or a greater depth of understanding. It can take us to a new place in the relationship from which we might make decisions. It can also help us see what's unique about the person, diminishing our tendency to use stereotypes of out-group members.

From my experience, relationship management is essential to negotiating power and its unequal impacts on social groups. Relationship management is more like a skill group than a single aptitude. It includes the ability to build trust, motivate, negotiate and work well with others, and deal effectively with disagreements and conflict.[6] It also builds on the inner skills of self-awareness, self-regulation, and empathy, supported by compassion.

Among the abilities that fall under relationship management is that of dealing with conflict. According to Diamond, "The skill of negotiating difference, at the heart of it, is a conflict skill because we have to navigate through different interests, positions, and stakes."[7] Diversity, at its core, is another word for difference. To negotiate difference we have to work though conflict, whether at the group or interpersonal level. And we also have to negotiate significant internal conflict, mental states in which we struggle consciously or unconsciously between incompatible needs, drives, impulses, or desires in relation to our in-groups and out-groups.

Diamond expands on this point in a practical way, highlighting the importance of making mistakes:

> There's a lot of uncertainty and difference in diversity; there's no way to be perfect at it. At some point you will make mistakes and you will be confronted by others. You are going to use the wrong term, you are unknowingly going to insult somebody and get corrected for doing so. You are going to be shamed—and for some people, this is really hard. They can never be wrong, there's too much shame and they shut down. Completely. One of the greatest skills is the ability to publicly say, "Oops, I got that wrong."

Effectively dealing with conflict allows us to get to a deeper level of understanding of other people, issues, and perspectives. We also learn about ourselves in the process. Paradoxically, conflict can serve to strengthen relationships between people and groups, and thereby, nurture healing. The key is for conflict to be handled well.

An Unexpected Response to Terrorism

I learned this lesson first-hand in a rather dramatic way. I was working in the Netherlands with young leaders on issues of racism and cultural integration. Our team had been invited to create a leadership program for the Dutch context, to tackle the thorny issues of multiculturalism, immigration, and belonging in post-9/11 Europe. This intercultural dialogue took place in 2005 in a retreat setting outside Amsterdam.

Nationalism was rising at the time, accompanied by anti-immigrant, anti-Muslim strife. The previous year, artist Theo van Gogh had been murdered in the streets of Amsterdam by an Islamic radical for making an inflammatory, anti-Islamic film and calling Muslims "goat-fuckers," among other choice racist slurs.[8] According to opinion polls, Islam, immigration, and integration had been at the top of Dutch minds since populist anti-immigration politician Pym Fortuyn was murdered in 2002 (surprisingly, by a white animal rights activist).

Feelings of "us" and "them" were intense in a society that lived significantly racially segregated realities. It was in this context that young leaders from across the country, aged seventeen to twenty-four, were invited to attend a two-week residential peace-building program. About 40 per cent were racial minorities and 60 per cent white; some participants had self-selected and others were sent by their organizations.

Our program, a precursor to the Deep Diversity framework, supported the participants on the levels of both head and heart. Intellectually, they were offered concepts that helped expand their understanding of race, discrimination, and social integration. We supported their hearts through activities that taught self-awareness, empathy, and the ability to name and express their emotions. There was an emphasis on relationship-building skills, including listening, communicating, and managing their emotional triggers.

We also offered several intergroup dialogue formats, including opportunities for white and racialized participants to share their experiences of belonging to, respectively, dominant and non-dominant groups. There were ample opportunities to talk about their experiences—perspective giving—and to listen to the experiences of others—perspective taking.

The conversations sometimes grew heated, eliciting painful experiences and exposing stark political divisions. Feelings of shame, anger, guilt, and pride were strongly expressed on both sides of the racial divide. This was our first year designing this program, and in spite of significant facilitation experience on our organizing team, we wondered at times if we had let it get off track.

The true test of relationships, however, came in an unexpected manner. On the second-last day of the program, we had just finished our Community Day. The young leaders had showcased their learning by teaching some key concepts to friends, family, community, and political officials. The event had gone extremely well. Participants demonstrated their new-found perspectives and camaraderie. They conducted themselves with grace and elegance, even in the presence of an inflammatory high-level politician whose caustic words promoted intolerance towards Dutch people who were black or Muslim. Our youth were on a high, and I felt very proud of them.

The date, however, was July 7, 2005. Just as Community Day was wrapping up, we received breaking news that the London Underground, less than an hour's flight from where we were, had been bombed. The world would later learn that four homegrown terrorists targeted the busy transit system with suicide bombs, killing fifty-two civilians along with themselves and injuring about seven hundred people. At the moment the news broke, we knew few details: only the destruction, smoke, death, and suspicions of a terrorist attack.

Our staff team struggled with what to do. We had limited media access in that remote location, and most of the participants did not even know the event had occurred.

We were worried that this news could derail everything we'd worked towards over the last two weeks. It could kill the spirit and, likely, split our community on the day before we were to depart—a terrible way to end the program. Our team, however, felt there was little choice. We had to share with the group what had happened and let the cards fall where they may.

We gathered all seventy youth leaders, and I apprehensively shared the news about London. Not knowing how else to proceed, we simply opened the floor to comments.

Rehana, a Moroccan Muslim, despaired: "9/11—it's happening again." Everyone in the room implicitly understood her fear of an anti-Islam backlash. As she wept, others nearby placed their hands on her, offering comfort.

A young white woman, Ingrid, shared that her sister was in London and was not responding to calls to her cell phone. Fearing the worst, Ingrid raced out of the room in tears. Remarkably, she was followed by Alisha, a young black woman, who went to comfort her. I say remarkable because these two women had been at loggerheads for the entire program, occupying opposing views on how racial minorities should or should not "integrate" into Dutch society. I thought they hated each other.

Abdul-Hamid, a former child soldier from East Africa, was completely distressed. His full scholarship to an Ivy League school was in jeopardy, he shared, as he now had a poor chance of obtaining a visa for the United States. Abdul-Hamid's goal was to use his education to help rebuild his war-torn country and support family members who still lived there. He put his head in his hands, trying to push back the tears. A large, lumbering white guy, Auke, protectively placed an arm around Abdul-Hamid's shoulders, offering silent support.

And so it went on spontaneously, without any intervention from the staff team. Participants took turns speaking from the heart, listening to each other, weeping, and offering each other what comfort they could.

It was the most remarkable and generous collective act of compassion and healing I've ever been a part of. As I walked around that evening, in many corridors I saw lit candles and small, diverse clusters of participants talking quietly, holding and supporting each other.

It took me a while to articulate what I was witnessing. And then the penny dropped: they were grieving. It was implicitly understood that "we" had been affected. There was no blame or finger pointing, except towards radical terrorists. There was no "us" or "them"—the loss was collective. This tragic event didn't split us along racial and religious lines, as I had feared. It brought us closer together. This group of participants did what all of our communities should have done, which was to grieve and mourn our collective losses.

A public act of terrorism was countered by a communal act of healing. I was overcome by this experience, by the compassion and deep learning it offered. It couldn't reverse the events, but it dramatically counteracted the reactionary responses heard in much of Europe.

Had this been the second day of the program rather than the second-last day, I'm certain this tragedy would have had a profoundly negative impact on the sense of community. Instead, the program became a testimony to the power of relationships—with the necessary head and heart skills in place at both interpersonal and intergroup levels—to effectively manage conflict and develop resilience.

Questions for Cultivating Relational and Conflict Skills

Many tools, books, training programs, and resources are available for developing relationship management and conflict skills. The following questions may serve as helpful starting points:

- Generally, how much attention and time do I spend helping and supporting others? How frequently do I ask, What can I do to help?
- How well do I listen? Do I both ask questions and fully attend to the responses? How frequently does my cell phone, tablet, or computer distract me during conversations or meetings?
- How skilled am I at noticing non-verbal communication in others and myself, including tone of voice, facial expressions, eye contact, posture, or gestures?
- How effective is my communication with others when I personally need help or support? Am I as clear as I could be?
- During disagreements or conflict, how skilled am I at standing up for myself and my own perspective? How easily do I let my position and needs go?
- How skilled am I at listening to the other person's perspective? Can I be curious and ask about their viewpoint, or do I get more entrenched in my position?
- How frequently do I invite feedback from other people? How well do I receive feedback (that may or may not be invited)?
- How aware am I of my own feelings and needs in relationships? How aware am I during disagreements or difficult situations?
- When things gets stressed and heated, how effectively do I manage my own emotions? How quickly can I regain a state of centred, calm clarity?

- When the situation becomes stressful or charged, or there is a clash of perspectives and experiences, how aware am I of the feelings and needs of others?
- Do I tend to avoid situations that are heated or filled with conflict? How willing am I to lean in to conflicts and explore ways of getting to understanding or resolution?
- How effective am I at working through disagreements or conflicting needs?

Review this list of questions again, but this time ask them in relation to social identity (race, gender, sexual orientation, ability, and so on). How well do I listen when issues of social identity are raised? How skilled am I at listening to the other person's perspective regarding race or gender issues?

Relational skills are significant markers of personal power. To transform conflict, we need to step beyond our perspective, and at times consider the issue from outside of our social identity. Sometimes, however, we face situations where conventional dialogue and conflict skills cannot be applied. The impacts of intergroup conflict can sometimes be so painful, personal, direct, historical, or complicated that there is no clear resolution.

In such cases, the best we can do is struggle to make sense of our lives and situations in some constructive manner. Meaning making, as we will see in the final chapter, is the inner skill that can help us move forward when nothing else can.

DEEP DIVERSITY: BRINGING IT ALL TOGETHER

Not Too Late

WAS INVITED to present at a youth leadership conference in Northern Ontario, where more than half of the participants were Aboriginal. After the presentation, I had planned to attend the screening of a video about Grassy Narrows First Nation, created by a youth group that was getting some buzz at the event. But I chose instead to continue a conversation with Walter, a teacher from Grassy Narrows with whom I was seated at lunch.

I'm glad I did. Walter spoke with great love and affection about his community. Yet the history of Grassy is filled with pain and anti-Aboriginal racism.[1] Government policy throughout the twentieth century, for example, forcibly took children from their families to live in the now infamous church-run residential schools, which worked to strip away the culture, language, and traditional ways of the Native people. As we know today, many of these institutions were rife with physical, emotional, and sexual abuse. Many people were damaged and some died, yet the community of Grassy Narrows survived.

In the 1960s, the people of Grassy were forced to relocate from their original territory—from their traditional subsistence lifestyle that was rich with fishing, hunting, and trapping—to make way for a hydroelectric project. The project destroyed a major food staple, wild rice beds, drowned out the fur-bearing animals that were central to their micro-economy, and flooded sacred burial grounds. They were forced to live on a reserve on a stagnant lake with poor soil that supports neither gardens nor their traditional ways. Yet, again, the people of Grassy adapted and survived, and continue to live there today.

In the 1970s, it was revealed that the fish were contaminated with mercury because of a paper mill upriver. The local fishing economy was destroyed overnight, with 90 per cent employment dropping to 10 per cent. Over a hundred deaths were recorded as a result of the mercury poisoning, called Minamata disease. (In 2010, scientists found that close to 60 per cent of the people of Grassy still have mercury-related ailments, including limited movement of limbs, loss of balance, hearing loss, insomnia, headaches, and fatigue. This includes people who were born long after the mercury dumping had ended.)[2]

Walter told the story of his community taking a downhill spiral as a result of choices, most of which were not their own. In such a context of neglect and poverty, it's not hard to understand why drug abuse, suicide, and various forms of physical and sexual violence took root. Walter also described how the community resisted and survived. He credited the women within this remarkable population for saving them through efforts to combat addictions when other avenues were closed.

To stop the clear-cutting of their treaty lands, Grassy Narrows First Nation mobilized. They began a campaign of road blockades in 2002, turning back logging trucks in spite of government and corporate opposition. (At the time of writing, the protest continues. Grassy Narrows is described as Canada's longest-running First Nations blockade.)[3]

Yet, what stands out for me most was what Walter said at the end of the conversation about Aboriginal peoples and the rest of Canada: "It's not too late, though."

"Not too late for what?" I asked.

"It's not too late for our relationship—there have been mistakes made on both sides."

Relationship? I struggled to see the "relationship" Walter referred to. Dishonouring of treaties. Forced relocation. Poisoning of the land. Destruction of culture. Abuse, poverty, and neglect. If anyone had reason to be angry and hold a militant position towards others, it was Walter.

His statement floored me. My eyes welled up, as I asked how he found it in his heart to say what he'd said, given the lopsidedness of historical events.

He quietly replied, "It's taken a lot of healing, brother, a lot of healing."

I still get goosebumps as I recall the story today. Walter had done something that I didn't understand very well at the time. His healing journey involved some powerful inner work that altered his perspective on the world. He was still fighting the good fight and was still part of the resistance efforts, such as the blockade to protect his community's land and rights. But he spoke of relationship. He spoke of reconciliation under circumstances where many of us might be drowning in despair and hate aimed at those who were the source of our persecution. He had healed enough that even those who might be considered his persecutors—whites, non-Aboriginals—were still worthy of relationship. He was able, under extremely difficult circumstances, to humanize his out-group.

Inner Skill 8: Making Meaning

Research on resilience reveals that those who are able to make meaning from negative situations in their lives are better able to bounce back from stress, tragedy, and trauma. In a 2008 study, Stephen Southwick and Dennis Charney from Yale University and their colleagues worked with former Vietnam prisoners of war, many of whom had been brutally tortured.[4] According to the research team, whose expertise is post-traumatic stress, most of these veterans had found ways to reinterpret the significance of their extremely harsh ordeal, having "grown stronger, wiser and more resilient as a result of it. They also reported that they were now better able to see possibilities for the future, relate to others and appreciate life."

To make meaning, we need to find constructive life lessons in adversity. Research with people who have suffered loss or trauma—including sexual abuse, rape, or death of a loved one—indicates the importance of being able to reflect on questions such as Why did this happen? and What good can come of it?[5] Those who wrote about their experiences and used these questions in their reflections seemed to recover and heal more quickly. Compared with peers who did not, they required less health care support over the following year.

Walter had clearly found a constructive way to make meaning of the extremely difficult experiences faced by his community, including overt and subtle forms of anti-Aboriginal racism. He spoke directly of having undergone a healing process to reach his state of compassion and forgiveness, and to keep his hand open to relationships with non-Aboriginals.

I offer Walter's story, and my meaning-making analysis, with two cautionary points. First, the healing process is a deeply individual, non-linear process. It depends on so many variables, including the availability of social supports, access to health care, genetic tendencies, and income and education levels. It's important to recognize that in some people's circumstances, it may be beyond their control—perhaps nearly impossible—to deal with their trauma. And so, we need to bring compassion rather than an expectation to heal to the forefront.

Second, my sharing of Walter's story arc is in no way meant to suggest that "racism is a good thing." That would be a gross misinterpretation. Racism is a horrible, crippling, and killing phenomenon that has intergenerational impacts. As anti-Aboriginal and anti-black racism suggests, in North America we are still living with the impacts of colonization and the transatlantic slave trade.

Yet racism is also a part of our human experience. And to change it, we first have to accept its reality and understand it. The initial anti-slavery campaigns started in the late 1700s, which means we've been working towards racial equality, in one form or another, for about 250 years. And our work is not done. Sometimes the more we learn, the more complicated things become. We now know that preferences for our in-groups have been neurologically hard-wired into our species—Homo sapiens—from the start, approximately 200,000 years ago. So what we're trying to undo, depending on what you consider the starting point, is somewhere between 200 and 200,000 years of history.

We are collectively still travelling along this incredible timeline. And much of the journey to end racism and nurture inclusion is similar for members of dominant and non-dominant groups. However, as we saw in the two chapters on power, the day-to-day realities and challenges faced by dominant and non-dominant people can be very different, whether we are aware of these differences or not. Therefore, it follows that the paths towards healing the racial rifts in society will also have to be somewhat different. Walter's story is one of a specific journey faced by a member of a non-dominant group. The following story of Francine will help us view things from a dominant group's perspective.

The First Step to Reconciliation

In the summer of 1990, a blockade was set up in Kanesatake, Native land of the mostly English-speaking Mohawks in the French-speaking province of Quebec, about an hour's drive from Montreal.[6] Once again, Aboriginal rights were being trampled. This time the scenario involved expansion plans for a golf course over ancestral burial grounds, pitting Mohawks against the town of Oka.

After spending a frustrating year going through official legal channels and protesting peacefully, Mohawks mobilized to protect their land. An armed standoff ensued with the provincial police, and eventually the army, which lasted almost three months. It was dramatic and tense, and a skirmish of gunfire occurred during a botched police raid on a Mohawk barricade. One police officer, Marcel Lemay, was shot and killed. His pregnant wife, two-year-old daughter, and sister, Francine, were bereaved. Photographs capturing solemn-faced Francine Lemay walking behind her thirty-one-year-old brother's casket were all over the news.

Fourteen years after the crisis, two university students asked Francine for her opinion on this historical event.[7] Embarrassed to have no opinion to offer, she read an account of the history of Oka. Curiously, the book that made it into her hands—*At the Woods' Edge*—was powerful but not well known, a self-published historical overview written by members of the Kanesatake community. It chronicled the Mohawk struggle to survive, including the betrayal of treaties and land rights that implicated both French and English governments and the church, which was to have held the land in trust but instead sold it off.[8]

Francine was shocked to confront this perspective on history. For example, she read of the relocation attempt in 1811 by the federal government. Mohawk families were promised food for the winter and seeds for the spring if they resettled far away in central Ontario. The families that went, however, were only given food for two weeks and lived in tents during the cold, hard winter. Many died of disease and hunger.

This version of historical events stood in stark opposition to what she learned as a child in francophone schools. Mohawks had been portrayed as the "bad Indians" for having supported the English during a pivotal historical period that led to the English victory over the region. The Huron, in contrast, who supported the French, were the "good Indians." Beyond that, her knowledge of Native history came from Hollywood movies.

"That book changed my life," Lemay told a news reporter. "It really touched my heart, to find out all the injustice, the pain and hurt, all the mistreatment [the Mohawks] received, and the inertia of the government."[9]

As a devout Christian, she struggled with the contradictions and gaps in her knowledge. As it happened, the same week she learned this new history, a delegation from Kanesatake was at her church to give a presentation about a project they were working on. During the event, Francine found herself shaking all over. Before it ended, she stood up in front of the congregation and asked to speak.

"I'm Marcel Lemay's sister, the police officer who got shot at Oka."

Pin drop silence.

"I want to apologize for the racist media and how the Mohawks have been treated."

Mavis Etienne, who had been a key negotiator during the Oka crisis, happened to be part of the Mohawk delegation. Mavis walked over to

OUTCOMES OF OKA

After a seventy-eight-day standoff, the Mohawk warriors eventually laid down their arms and surrendered. Marcel Lemay's killer, however, was never identified, and the golf course was never built. The cost to taxpayers was more than $180 million (not including the cost of the army). In 1997, the federal government purchased the disputed land from the village of Oka, and the Mohawk community was allowed to expand their cemetery. A key player in the crisis at the time, Quebec Native Affairs Minister John Ciaccia, would say twenty years later that "the whole crisis could have been avoided with common sense and respect for the native community."

Source:
"Oka Crisis Legacy Questioned," CBC News, www.cbc.ca, July 11, 2010.

Francine and hugged her, offering condolences for the loss of her brother.

Could there have been a dry eye in the house?

This was a powerful moment of reconciliation. It would be the first of many steps Francine would take towards healing with the Mohawk people of Kanesetake. Mavis invited Francine to attend an ecumenical gathering to commemorate the Oka crisis, called the Trail of Prayers. Francine went. When the trail ended in the Pines, the site of her brother's death, Francine was overtaken by nausea and weakness. Though she was invited to leave if she needed to, Francine insisted on completing the ceremony.

Francine described this experience as "the first phase of my healing . . . I let myself mourn my brother—for the first time."[10] This was in 2004, almost a decade and a half after Marcel's death.

Francine began occasionally attending Mavis Etienne's church in Kanesatake. She also realized that many friends in her francophone community in Montreal still held old ideas and prejudices. Mohawks were stereotypically referred to as savages, and as involved in "illegal cigarettes, the bingos, the lottery."[11] She decided she could do something to help educate her fellow Quebecers: translate *At the Woods' Edge* into French. Translation was her profession, and this was her way of giving something back.

The offer was met with surprise, joy, and even some discomfort from the Mohawk community. But they accepted her offer, and she toiled away for nine months until the book was successfully translated. *À l'Orée des Bois* was available in time for the twentieth anniversary of the Oka crisis.

"This is like my contribution for the pain the Mohawks endured throughout the centuries, my way to make amends," she explained. "The first step to reconciliation is knowledge, information. So I have to inform the Québécois, the Francophones about the history of Kanesatake."[12]

A Dominant Group Member's Journey

Francine, being white, needed to go through a process of learning and unlearning. It started with her knowledge of historical events. Her teachers had taught her a skewed version of history, one that stereotyped Mohawks as savages, whose only role was to take a side in the "more important" struggle between two dominant European powers. The assumption was that Indigenous peoples have no important place in history or contemporary society on their own merit and should only be discussed in reference to one of Canada's "founding" nations. A problematic assumption, to say the least.

This, of course, is not about Francine or her local context. Most non-Aboriginal people are taught this version of history through both formal (schools) and informal (news, movies) education sources. The power to write, tell, and reinforce history is a formidable manifestation of institutional power. It was something that Francine took for granted until she started to expand her knowledge of history through another perspective.

Francine modelled the use of key inner skills and took a number of important steps that are relevant for dominant group members.

- *Self-awareness:* Although Francine was prompted by two students who wanted her opinion on Oka, she had enough self-awareness to realize that she didn't know very much about the topic. That required significant humility.

- *Self-regulation:* Her brother had died. To be asked an opinion about an incident that is so emotionally loaded and not just lash out, point fingers, and verbally attack those she might have held responsible took willpower and fortitude. On the flip side, Francine could also have shut down emotionally, suppressing and avoiding the issue altogether. Managing her emotions and psychological state in a constructive way enabled her to move forward. It also speaks to a level of inner power she already possessed.

- *Self-education:* Francine could easily have relied on stereotypes and media sound bites to make sense of things during that hot Oka summer. Instead, she had a deep desire to learn more. Her curiosity was coupled with being open to a new perspective on history—one that challenged, and even implicated, her white, European, Christian roots. She could easily have taken a defensive posture, dismissed what she was reading, and found resources about Oka that supported her established views and position. But she remained open and curious, instead of reactive, again a testament to her inner strength.

- *Empathy and relationship building:* Things could have ended at self-education, but Francine went beyond that. She spoke out publicly, demonstrating empathy for the historical and current struggles of the Mohawk people. In a profound act of reconciliation, she apologized, when it was she who had lost a brother. This triggered another series of events, including apologies from Mohawk representatives. Eventually, she would be able to authentically grieve the loss of her sibling. The ongoing relationship continued with her act of solidarity with the Mohawk people. She translated the book that had educated her into French, as a way of combatting stereotypes and educating her own people.

- *Meaning making:* Marcel Lemay's killer was never identified nor brought to justice. Francine had to find some way to make sense of her life and of her brother's death. Her strong roots in the Christian tradition helped her in some important ways, including her awareness that she needed to forgive. For example, she had gone to Oka shortly after her brother's death to let the Mohawks know she forgave them, but at that time she was not allowed to cross the police line.[13] Later, Francine acknowledged it had been an inauthentic attempt—if felt more like something she should do as a good Christian. Her first true grieving happened fourteen years later, when she broke down during the Trail of Prayers ceremony. She had to wrestle with those demons, even as she reached out to, and was supported by, the Mohawk community. But her reflections indicate that she found a specific way to make meaning that provides some solace. "You cannot measure someone's pain. I cannot say my pain is greater than what the Mohawks went through, through centuries of abuse," she said during a radio interview, her voice sounding reflective. "But through his death, I found friends."[14]

A Non-dominant Group Member's Journey

Walter's story is intimately tied to the journey of Grassy Narrows. I don't want to speculate on his personal struggles. But at the least, he was a witness to the decline in his community's choices and possibilities due to various levels of government intervention (or lack thereof) and the rise of destructive elements such as mercury poisoning, unemployment, and addictions. His life was definitely touched in some way, directly or indirectly, by living in a small community that survived such difficult challenges as forced relocation, Minamata disease, and destruction of traditional ways of life. Many direct and indirect influences from outside Grassy Narrows can be seen as sources of the negative events and changes in the community's history.

Yet Walter did not hate whites or non-Aboriginal people. Instead he spoke of reconciliation, healing, and relationship. Although the qualities he possessed are similar to Francine's, they come from a different perspective, that of a non-dominant group member. We have fewer details of Walter's story, but we can still identify significant aspects of his journey.

- *Meaning making:* Walter had to make some sense out of the pain that he and his community experienced. Yet when I spoke to him, he wasn't despairing. He spoke with great love, admiration, and respect for Grassy Narrows. He exemplified what it means to be able to see both the beauty and the brutality in the world. He knew the challenges in his community better than anyone. His serenity communicated that he accepted what could not be changed. Equally, by his presence on his community's blockade and pride in their success at resisting logging trucks, he showed a willingness to fight for what could be changed. When speaking with me, he neither sugar-coated the struggles nor drowned in despair. His equanimity and wisdom left me feeling I had met a true elder (although I don't know whether he held that title in his community). A long tradition of healing circles, ceremonies, and other modalities within Aboriginal communities can support such healing and the development of inner power.
- *Empathy and relationship building:* Walter's statement was simple and explicit: "It's not too late for our relationship—there have been mistakes made on both sides." In spite of a lopsided history and an unbalanced dynamic of political and economic power, Walter was willing to take responsibility for mistakes made on his people's side of the relationship. This, too, is a powerful marker of reconciliation. It's a complementary gesture to Francine's apology to the Mohawks, in spite of the loss of her brother.
- *Self-awareness and self-regulation:* Given that Grassy Narrows had been hit with multiple tragedies over many generations, it's not difficult to imagine a person becoming angry, vengeful, violent, or despairing and self-destructive. To be hopeful and whole, Walter had to learn to notice and manage his feelings, to grieve, to express, and to heal. This required him to gain insight into his own behaviour and choices and to be able to self-regulate.

As discussed in the chapters on power, an awareness of historical injustices can make anger, self-destruction, and distrust the driving feelings for many people. Yet these same feelings of victimization—feelings that may help mobilize around a cause in the short term—can be a defence mechanism for a deeper level of grief and shame that needs to be named and processed in order to heal. It's clear that Walter had delved into these depths and come out the other side, which required great self-knowledge and personal power.

- *Self-education:* Walter had a very personal relationship to Grassy Narrows that he was able to put into a broader context. Non-dominant groups can develop negative evaluations of themselves—in this case, internalizing an anti-Aboriginal bias. But being curious about history and understanding the political and economic forces at play—understanding power dynamics—can help bring compassion for one's situation. In the case of a community like Grassy Narrows, it's not hard to imagine that despair and feelings of inadequacy could set in. When struggles are placed into a broader context, the results can be empowering. Walter had knowledge that allowed him to see both the positives and negatives of Grassy Narrows. He could also acknowledge mistakes made on the side of his own people, even if the balance was lopsided, a further empowering step to fight an attitude of victimization.

Both Walter's and Francine's stories hold many powerful lessons on moving forward from horrifying loss and traumatic racial conflict in an authentic manner. Those lessons go well beyond what has been articulated here. Their experiences may best serve as inspiration rather than recipe. There are no clean lines or steps for recovery or meaning making. It's a deeply individual process that is messy, painful, and uncertain. Perhaps just knowing that we have to reach both outwards to others and inwards into ourselves may serve as a starting point.

Intergroup tensions and issues of racial difference are never-ending processes of learning, unlearning, and transformation. A willingness to engage in this process can be painful, but it can also bear fruit in unique ways. It may, at times, permanently shift our attitudes and worldviews, making things better for others and ourselves.

Learning New Implicit Habits

My partner, Annahid, and I were processing our marriage licence at one side of the entrance to city hall. Given the four cultural and three religious traditions of our families, we had decided to do a multistep process of "tying the knot," inviting the Muslim, Christian, Hindu, Persian, British, Indian, and Pakistani aspects of our ancestry into a self-designed ceremony (Oh, Canada!). She and I had discussed for many months how to navigate all the competing needs—including our own. We were doing a decent job of juggling the essentials, in spite of dropping a few balls. We had just completed an official civil service on an upper floor of city hall, the first of four ceremonies to take place over a month-long extravaganza of related events.

The administrator, a white woman who looked fifty-something and spoke with a Scottish brogue, was helping us get through a legal hurdle: the paperwork. Upon completion of the appropriate forms, she turned to Annahid, smiled warmly, and shook her hand.

"Congratulations," she said emphatically. "You're now officially married!" Without missing a beat, the woman turned to me and asked in the most genuine, easeful manner, "Do you shake hands?"

"Yes," I replied, slightly surprised at the question.

"Well, congratulations!" she said and shook my hands with equal warmth and kindness.

I never got the woman's name, but that experience has stayed with me. Not because the signing of our marriage papers was memorable—it's a simple bureaucratic procedure, after all—but because of what this woman taught me about diversity and inclusion. Let me explain.

I had completed the paperwork first. After Annahid signed to "seal the deal," the administrator immediately congratulated her with a handshake.

As a bureaucrat who deals with the careful registration of names, she likely did some quick mental calculus. First, guessing that my name might be Muslim in origin, and second, knowing that some Muslim men don't shake hands with women. Instead of feeling thrown off by this knowledge, she confronted the uncertainty head-on by asking me a straightforward question: Do you shake hands?

Although the question surprised me, it was asked with the utmost ease and comfort. It was clear by the administrator's body language, tone, and mannerisms that she would have been completely comfortable had my response been yes or no.

She demonstrated what is sometimes referred to as the Platinum Rule in the world of inclusion, diversity, and equity: *Treat others the way they want to be treated.* (Rather than, as the Golden Rule many of us have learned puts it, the way *you* want to be treated).

As discussed previously, shaking hands is such a cultural habit that we may not think twice about it. For many people in mainstream North America—myself included—being uncertain about shaking hands with another person can create feelings of discomfort and anxiety, both consciously and unconsciously. We prefer to avoid feelings associated with making mistakes or doing things wrong. Our shame buttons can get pressed, which usually means anger and resentment are not far behind.

This administrator's actions and attitude demonstrated what it means to learn a new cultural habit. And, given her age, she also exemplified that learning is a life-long process. Many of us old folks can, in fact, learn new tricks.

Somewhere along the way, she had decided it was important to unlearn a long-ingrained habit (assuming that shaking hands was "normal" for everyone) and learn a new practice (asking the question, if she suspected it might be an issue). She was specifically welcoming conservative Muslims in this case, although there are other cultural groups who share the same practice. She had made a choice to become conscious of something that most people take for granted.

That subtle but extremely important step is what the bulk of the Deep Diversity framework is about: changing habits. To nurture inclusion, diversity, and equity, we have to become aware of unconscious behavioural patterns. We have to become more aware of circumstances where such default tendencies do not serve our relationship with others, especially those we perceive to be different than ourselves.

Skill Development

So how can we systematize the skills of the marriage licence administrator? By drawing on the four pillars of Deep Diversity. Here are some suggestions for becoming more conscious in our interactions with others to maximize the possibility of inclusive and fair interactions.

- *Bias:* Accept the fact that all of us have implicit biases. Such biases are normal neurological processes that are both helpful (to filter and prioritize input) and harmful (stereotypes, favouritism). As individuals, we must all be on the lookout for how our biases manifest and catch ourselves in the act. We can use our conscious mind to detect, decode, and diminish how bias plays out for us and for those around us. Remember, the less we are aware of bias, the larger a role it will have in our interactions with others. Notice the actions and attitudes of people that decrease feelings of inclusion, and track and build upon those that promote inclusion. Use the bias reduction skills outlined in chapter 3.
- *Tribes:* Notice the social identities and groups in our context, from those that have the greatest rank and power to those that have the least. As individuals, we must become aware of belonging to dominant or non-dominant groups, and notice the subtle and not-so-subtle ways in which people interact with each other based on these social identities. Notice the people or groups on the margins, and see if there are patterns that keep people on the outside based on social identity (race, gender, class, sexual orientation, ability, and so on). Also, notice the positive interactions and the behaviour of people who are trying to build bridges

across differences, in both subtle and systemic ways. Incorporate these behaviours into our repertoire and build on them.

- *Power:* Notice how rank and power dynamics manifest in our personal, professional, or community lives. Notice how many dominant groups and non-dominant groups we as individuals belong to. Take an inventory of both our social and personal power. How do rank and power play out in our workplaces? What are individuals, leaders, and organizations doing that demonstrate the positive use of rank and power, in ways that increase a sense of community, inclusion, and diversity? Incorporate these practices and be a positive role model for others. Also notice how people use power negatively or badly, and try to avoid those practices. Discuss with others how we personally use power in our personal or professional lives, examining both our strengths and weaknesses.

- *Emotions:* Develop deeper levels of self-awareness—what we're individually feeling on a moment-to-moment basis. This awareness gives us greater choice in what to do, say, and think. As discussed in chapter 2, all our interactions with other people are emotional to a greater or lesser degree, in either positive or negative ways. Emotions are powerful and they usually drive our behaviour and choices. The less we are aware of how we feel, the greater a role emotions have in our lives. Emotions play an especially powerful role in our interactions with members of other groups—the less familiarity we have with out-group members, the greater our anxiety, fear, and use of stereotypes. Attempting to uncover bias or explore rank and power issues is truly emotion-filled terrain. To enhance diversity and inclusion, it is essential to developing the self-awareness and self-regulation techniques for handling how we feel.

No matter how we slice it, the outcome is the same. The less we are aware of the unconscious dynamics of emotions, bias, tribes, and power, the more impact they have in our lives.

It takes some effort for us to get along on a planet of seven billion people. The multiple dimensions of the Deep Diversity lens can assist. The marriage licence administrator, for one, employed all four aspects of the Deep Diversity framework.

- *Tribes:* First, she recognized that to do her job well, she needed to tune in to the needs of members of other groups, especially those who are historically non-dominant, some of whom may have different habits than she was accustomed to.

- *Emotions:* She mastered her emotions and opted to be curious rather than anxious, angry, or resentful about the need to accommodate, challenging her own assumptions about handshakes with members of the opposite sex. She also likely had to go through a series of interactions where she was less successful and more awkward—this is true anytime we learn something new—and, again, dealt with the feelings related to failure. Rather than giving up, denouncing, or demanding that "they" conform to "our" standards, she stood firm in her commitment to learning and was resilient enough to develop a new way of doing things.

- *Bias:* In taking a new approach, she also had to tackle the preference or bias of her in-group, which would have predisposed her to think about a "right" versus "wrong" way of congratulating someone.

- *Power:* Finally, there was an implicit and explicit use of power to create positive outcomes for everyone involved, including herself. She mobilized positional power within the institution to help create a more welcoming interaction and experience for non-dominant groups. With or without intention, she used her dominant group identity as a white person to be an ally to a non-dominant group member, leveraging her higher racial rank to create an inclusive interaction. The inner work she did to create a new way of doing things—including being curious, managing her emotions, going through a learning curve, and making mistakes—

required the use of her personal power. The results came across in the ease with which she interacted with me regarding the hand-shake. The outcomes also benefit her. She is more comfortable and can tilt towards (rather than away from) interactions with out-group members. Further, her fluidity in dealing with new-ness coincidentally notches up her personal power.

We're talking about changing our habits at the implicit level. It's very subtle but extremely important work. Our implicit bias and attitudes towards our in-groups—especially if we are from the dominant racial group—lead to unfairness and inequality in society. From seemingly inno-cent preferences such as which stranger we choose to sit beside on public transit, to critical issues in health care and policing that can result in people losing their lives, our implicit bias and related unconscious habits play a significant role.

The Deep Diversity lens can help us name, talk about, and navigate systemic discrimination. Asking the four gateway questions can help us uncover those issues that may be more hidden or unconscious:

- What are the influences of emotions in this situation, group, or issue?
- What are the influences of bias?
- What are the influences of tribes?
- What are the influences of power?

The related skills—self-awareness, self-regulation, empathy, relation-ship management, and conflict skills—are the critical inner work tools we need to sharpen on this journey. Meditation is the practice that can deepen our inner skills, and compassion is the hidden fuel needed to enhance our ability to make and accept the mistakes that necessarily have to be made as we learn about others.

A Final Word

Racism remains a defining issue in our world, and tackling it on a systemic level is more subtle and tricky than confronting its more overt manifestations. But we all need to make meaning of something that is inherently awful, unfair, and at times, violent.

I have grappled with the themes of prejudice and discrimination for twenty years now, as a teacher, consultant, and life-long student. And I continue to struggle with them. There is no perfect answer to racism, but this book outlines my thinking so far. (And I'm sure I've raised more questions than I've answered.)

When I'm really in a difficult emotional place because something terrible has happened—like the terrorist attack in Paris just before this book was completed (see sidebar: Paris Terrorist Attack)—I try to put this work into a historical context.

We are here because of all those who came before us—because of the trials, tribulations, mistakes, and successes of our ancestors. The civil rights movement tore through the poisonous outer bark of racism. As a result, overt forms of discrimination are rejected by the mainstream today.

Enough has changed that a black man with humble beginnings has become the president of the United States. But our work is not complete. Perhaps, like democracy, it is a project with no real end. Perhaps it is only a series of ongoing steps we take, with improvements and renovations outweighing the setbacks. We inherited this responsibility from our elders, and we must continue moving it forward.

I also draw on my belief that we, as a species, are learners. We have changed our thinking and behaviours and will continue to do so. We are far from where we need to be, but certainly further ahead than when I was born in the late 1960s.

In fact, I recall attending a lecture in Toronto about fifteen years ago by Noam Chomsky, the prominent thinker and cultural icon, where someone asked him this very question: "Is the world better or worse since you started your work?" He was in his early seventies at that time, and his answer was

PARIS TERRORIST ATTACK: ENTRENCHING US/THEM

In January 2015, a terrorist attack in Paris took place with the cold-blooded murder of ten journalists—mostly staff from the satirical magazine *Charlie Hebdo*—and two police officers. A massive manhunt ensued, resulting in the death of the suspected killers, two brothers raised in France who self-identified as part of the radical, so-called Islamic group, al-Qaida in Yemen. This, according to reports, was revenge for how the cartoonists made fun of the Prophet Mohammed, the religion's central figure who represents the words of God.

Peaceful protests took place worldwide under the hashtag "Je suis Charlie," with the ensuing debate framed as a freedom of speech issue. On the heels of this incident were discussions about how to prevent the radicalization of Muslim youth in Western nations.

Suffice it to say, rather than breakthroughs, the sense of Us versus Them was amplified by the many sides of this complex issue.

an unequivocal "Yes, it's better." He then went on to recite numerous examples since he was a young lad, including the development of vaccines that save millions of lives annually, creation of structures of global co-operation such as the United Nations, expansion of literacy and journalism worldwide, the progress made on gender and race, the reduction of crime in both nations, and the decline in the number of conflicts globally.

The audience in the room seemed to sigh in relief at this answer. Since then, I've encountered others who have expressed similar ideas, including Steve Pinker from Harvard University, who has written considerably on this topic,[15] as well His Holiness the Dalai Lama.[16]

Most of us, however, feel the opposite. With Ebola, terrorist attacks, cyberbullying, ISIS, the Israel-Palestine conflict, police shootings, and sexual assault, there's good reason to feel discouraged, even hopeless. Yet, this is mostly a trick of negativity bias. Both our internal predisposition and the external force of media sources emphasize bad rather than good news.

When I am overwhelmed by events or frustrated that change is not happening quickly enough, I try to zoom out and take a bird's-eye view of this shared journey we are on. From this vantage point, we're advancing. I also recall that the ratio of blood, sweat, and tears has shifted. Less blood is required than in our ancestors' time. But an unending supply of sweat and tears is needed to continue this crazy project of improving fairness and equality in society.

Democracy is just straight-up hard work. Tackling our unconscious biases and habits is the next big step we collectively need to take. Compassion is the driving force for me—as well as understanding that I am a small part of a journey that started long before I got here and will continue long after I am gone. This is not a sprint, but an ultra-marathon, spanning generations.

At least, that is how I make constructive sense of my involvement in the work on race, diversity, and our differences.

If you haven't already done so, you're invited into your personal meaning-making project, whether you're racialized, white, or Aboriginal. My deepest desire is that in some small way, this book will help you constructively deal with our shared challenges.

Salaam. Namaste.

ACKNOWLEDGEMENTS

Similarly to child-rearing, it takes a village to raise a writer. In the three-year process of writing *Deep Diversity*, many people have helped me both directly and indirectly.

I'd like to start by thanking Amanda Crocker and all the staff at Between the Lines, for believing in the contents of *Deep Diversity* when it was only a pitch on paper, for taking a risk on an unknown writer, and for patiently waiting for me to finish way beyond the original timeframe. Gratitude to Mary Newberry for being such a brilliant editor for the structure and content, helping turn my Frankenstein mess into something that was eminently more readable and coherent. I also want to acknowledge Tilman Lewis, who not only made my snaggle-toothed text consistent and flowing through his wonderful copy edit, but also patiently answered all of my grammar questions—the ones I never bothered to learn from my English teachers.

There were many early readers who gave their input into my primitive drafts, helping me identify what was working and what was not. This includes thanks to Barb Thomas, Chris Hayward, Deborah Barndt, Indy Batth, Irfan Toor, Janet Dashtgard, Jerry Brodey, James Orbinski, Julie Devaney, Judy Rebick, Lynn Heath, Monika Choudhury, Parker Johnson, Sheelagh Davis, and Sandy Yep.

Gratitude to the Downey-Gordon household—specifically Dave, Debbie, and Madison—who are not just fabulous neighbours, but provided invaluable guidance in developing a media/outreach strategy for the book.

Appreciations to the people who read the book, endorsed it, and then opened their networks to me in the U.S., including Robert Gass, Rinku Sen, Geraldine Paredez Vasquez, and Colleen Butler. Special thanks to Tonya Surman at the Centre for Social Innovation, Karen Rolston and Joenita Paulrajan at the Centre for Intercultural Communication at the University of British Columbia, as well as Steve Law at the Tatamagouche Centre for their enthusiastic support for the book and its launches.

A big shout-out to Julie Diamond—a sweetheart of a person if there ever was one—for being in so many conversations with me regarding the dynamics of power and social activism as well as doing a psychology check on the book's content. On a similar note, cheers to Eddy Nason for identifying certain dodgy bits during the science check, forcing me to go back and take another look.

Thanks also to the researchers who provided background on their work, including Kerry Kawakami at York University and Michael Inzlicht at the University of Toronto Scarborough as well as author/psychologist Rick Hanson, founder of the Wellspring Institute for Neuroscience and Contemplative Wisdom.

I'm profoundly grateful to Mahzarin Banaji at Harvard, who took the time out of her outlandish schedule not only to meet with me, but also to provide detailed notes on my book. You are not just a ground-breaker and inspiration in the field of bias research, but a truly generous soul!

The unsung hero of this writing project is James Beaton, our office manager at Anima Leadership and a dear friend. He did what he always does, which is to handle the behind-the-scenes work tirelessly and without complaint, including being researcher extraordinaire and sounding board for my undeveloped ideas. Deep appreciation for being my right hand during this project.

Thanks also to my tightknit family for all the thousands of small and large expressions of support, including childcare, making meals, and celebrating the project milestones. This includes my mom and dad, Saeeda and Anil Choudhury, sisters Bipasha and Monika, brother-in-law Sundeep, as well as my nephews Zephan and Dastan.

And, lastly, I am indebted to my partner in both life and business, Annahid Dashtgard. Throughout this endeavour she was the voice of positivity, encouraging me through thick and thin to write the book. Even when we hit tough moments, and I was crabby or graceless, Annahid never questioned the importance of the project or the time it was taking. She is a fearless advocate for the book and its contents, more than I can ever be. Thanks for your generosity and patience, for tending the home fire and lovingly looking after the kids while I was in my writing cave.

NOTES

CHAPTER 1. THE FOUR PILLARS OF DEEP DIVERSITY

1 Names in these case studies are most often pseudonyms.

2 K. Kawakami, E. Dunn, F. Karmali, and J.F. Dovidio, "Mispredicting Affective and Behavioral Responses to Racism," *Science* 323 (2009), 276–78.

3 Shakil Choudhury, interview with K. Kawakami, Toronto: York University, Department of Psychology, Oct. 18, 2012.

4 Thomas Lewis, Fari Amini, and Richard Lannon, *A General Theory of Love* (New York: Vintage Books, 2000), 35–65.

5 Ibid., 36.

6 Matthew D. Lieberman, *Social: Why Our Brains Are Wired to Connect* (New York: Crown Publishers, 2013), 39–54.

7 Mahzarin R. Banaji and Anthony G. Greenwald, *Blind Spot: Hidden Biases of Good People* (New York: Delacorte Press, 2013), 32–52.

8 M.R. Banaji and R. Bhaskar, "Implicit Stereotypes and Memory: The Bounded Rationality of Social Beliefs," in *Memory, Brain, and Belief*, ed. D.L. Schacter and E. Scarry (Cambridge, MA: Harvard University Press, 2000), 139–75.

9 Brian A. Nosek, Mahzarin R. Banaji, and Anthony G. Greenwald, "Harvesting Implicit Group Attitudes and Beliefs from a Demonstration Web Site," *Group Dynamics: Theory, Research, and Practic* 6,1 (2002), 101–115.

10 Jennifer N. Gutsell and Michael Inzlicht, "Empathy Constrained: Prejudice Predicts Reduced Mental Simulation of Actions during Observation of Outgroups," *Journal of Experimental Social Psychology* 46 (2010), 841–45.

11 "Human Brain Recognizes and Reacts to Race," *ScienceDaily*, www.sciencedaily.com, April 7, 2010.

12 Konrad Yakabuski, "Trayvon's Killing Echoes an Uglier Time in America," *The Globe and Mail* (Toronto), March 30, 2013.

13 Tom Blackwell, "Ferguson Mayor Says He Was Unaware of Racial 'Frustrations' in Community until Michael Brown Shooting," *National Post*, www.nationalpost.com, Nov. 26, 2014.

14 Frank Newport, "Blacks, Nonblacks Hold Sharply Different Views of Martin Case: Blacks More Likely to Believe Race Is a Major Factor," *Gallup*, www.gallup.com, April 5, 2012.

15 Maureen J. Brown, *We Are Not Alone: Police Racial Profiling in Canada, the United States, and the United Kingdom* (Toronto: African Canadian Community Coalition on Racial Profiling, 2004), 9.

16 Jonathan Haidt, *The Happiness Hypothesis: Finding Modern Truth in Ancient Wisdom* (New York: Basic Books, 2006), 43.

17 Feng Sheng and Shihui Han, "Manipulations of Cognitive Strategies and Intergroup Relationships Reduce the Racial Bias in Empathic Neural Responses," *NeuroImage* 61 (2012), 786–97.

18 Dora Capozza, Luca Andrighetto, Gian Antonio Di Bernardo, and Rosella Falvo, "Does Status Affect Intergroup Perceptions of Humanity?," *Group Process & Intergroup Relations* 15,3 (2012), 363–77.

19 David Dobbs, "Mastery of Emotions," *Scientific American Mind* (Feb./March 2006), 48.

20 Ibid., 44–49.

21 Daniel J. Siegel, *Mindsight: The New Science of Personal Transformation* (New York: Bantam Books Trade Paperbacks, 2011), 133.

22 Ibid., 198–200.

23 Harold Garfinkel, *Studies in Ethnomethodology* (Cambridge, UK: Polity Press, 1991), 36.

24 Banaji and Bhaskar, "Implicit Stereotypes and Memory," 142–43.

25 Siegel, *Mindsight*, 24–25.

26 Haidt, *The Happiness Hypothesis*, 37–38.

27 Beck Institute for Cognitive Behavior Therapy, "Cognitive Therapy Can Treat," www.beckinstitute.org.

28 Rick Hanson, *Buddha's Brain: The Practical Neuroscience of Happiness, Love and Wisdom* (Oakland, CA: New Harbinger Publications, 2009), 2–3.

29 Lorne Ladner, *The Lost Art of Compassion: Discovering the Practice of Happiness in the Meeting of Buddhism and Psychology* (San Francisco: HarperCollins, 2004), 14.

30 Edith Eisler, "Yo-Yo Ma: On the Silk Road," *All Things Strings* (May/June 2001), www.allthingsstrings.com.

CHAPTER 2. EMOTIONS

1   Town of Herouxville, http://welcome-to-herouxville-quebec-canada.blogspot.ca.

2   Marion Scott, "Islamophobia Surging in Quebec since Charter, Group Says: 117 Complaints of Verbal, Physical Abuse Made between Sept. 15 and Oct. 15 Compared with 25 Total for Previous Nine Months," *Montreal Gazette*, Nov. 6, 2013.

3   Lewis, Amini, and Lannon, *A General Theory of Love*, 3.

4   Daniel Goleman, "What Makes a Leader?," *Harvard Business Review* (Jan. 2004), http://hbr.org.

5   Daniel Goleman, Richard E. Boyatsis, and Annie McKee, *Primal Leadership: Learning to Lead with Emotional Intelligence* (Boston: Harvard Business Press, 2002, 2004), 28.

6   Haidt, *The Happiness Hypothesis*, 12.

7   Paul Rozin and Edward B. Royzman, "Negativity Bias, Negativity Dominance, and Contagion," *Personality and Social Psychology Review* 5,4 (2001), 296–320.

8   Hanson, *Buddha's Brain*, 40–42.

9   Lewis, Amini, and Lannon, *A General Theory of Love*, 41.

10 Eunice Yang, David H. Zald, and Randolph Blake, "Fearful Expressions Gain Preferential Access to Awareness during Continuous Flash Suppression," *Emotion* 7,4 (Nov. 2007), 882–86.

11 Jennifer Eberhardt, "Imaging Race," *American Psychologist* 60,2 (Feb./March 2005), 181–90.

12 City of Brampton Economic Development Office, "National Household Survey Bulletin #1: Immigration, Citizenship, Place of Birth, Language, Ethnic Origin, Visible Minorities, Religion, and Aboriginal Peoples," www.brampton.ca, May 2013.

13 San Grewal, "Brampton Suffers Identity Crisis as Newcomers Swell City's Population," *Toronto Star*, May 24, 2013.

14 Ingrid Peritz, "Quebec Mayor Tips His Cap at Francophone Muslim Immigrants," *The Globe and Mail* (Toronto), March 17, 2011, A9.

15 Goleman, Boyatzis, and McKee, *Primal Leadership*, 5–6.

16 Lewis, Amini, and Lannon, *A General Theory of Love*, 64–65.

17 Sigal Barsade, "Faster Than a Speeding Text: 'Emotional Contagion' at Work," *Psychology Today*, www.psychologytoday.com, Oct. 15, 2014.

18 Lewis, Amini, and Lannon, *A General Theory of Love*, 78–96.

19 Matthew D. Lieberman, *Social: Why Our Brains Are Wired to Connect* (New York: Crown Publishers, 2013), 40.

20 Ibid., 57–59.

21 Kipling D. Williams, "The Pain of Exclusion," *Scientific American Mind* (Jan./Feb. 2011), 30–37.

22 Goleman, Boyatzis, and McKee, *Primal Leadership*, 14.

23 Ibid., 12–14.

24 William Cara, "Perspective on Labour and Income: The Online Edition," *Statistics Canada* 4,6 (June 2003).

25 Goleman, Boyatzis, and McKee, *Primal Leadership*, 5–15.

26 Kevin Dougherty, "Multiculturalism 'Idiocy,' Charges Anti-Immigration Crusader," *Montreal Gazette*, May 20, 2011.

27 Canadian Immigrant Report, "CIReport.ca Interviews: André Drouin," www.cireport.ca, Sept 16, 2011.

28 Ingrid Peritz, "How Is the Controversial Charter of Values Going over in the Quebec Heartland?," *The Globe and Mail*, www.theglobeandmail.com, Sept. 20, 2013.

29 Lewis, Amini, and Lannon, *A General Theory of Love*, 20–33.

30 Ibid.

31 Frank Krueger et al., "The Neural Bases of Key Competencies of Emotional Intelligence," *Proceedings of the National Academy of Sciences* 106,52 (2009), 22486–91.

32 Haidt, *The Happiness Hypothesis*, 29–34.

33 Hanson, *Buddha's Brain*, 96–97.

34 Jaclyn Ronquillo et al., "The Effects of Skin Tone on Race-Related Amygdala Activity: An fMRI Investigation," *Social Cognitive and Affective Neuroscience* 2 (2007), 39–44.

35 Hanson, *Buddha's Brain*, 101.

36 Siegel, *Mindsight*, xi–xii.

37 Lewis, Amini, and Lannon, *A General Theory of Love*, 41–42.

38 Tiffany A. Ito and Bruce D. Bartholow, "The Neural Correlates of Race," *Trends in Cognitive Sciences* 13,12 (2009), 524–30.

39 Max Weisbuch, Kristin Pauker, and Nalini Ambady, "The Subtle Transmission of Race Bias via Televised Nonverbal Behavior," *Science* 326 (Dec. 2009), 1711–14.

40 Joseph Hall, "TV Clips Reveal Racist Body Language, Study Finds," *Toronto Star*, www.thestar.com, Dec. 18, 2009.

41 Shakil Choudhury, interview with Michael Inzlicht, Sept. 17, 2012.

42 Goleman, Boyatzis, and McKee, *Primal Leadership*, 40–45.

43 Ibid., 40.

44 Siegel, *Mindsight*, ix–xii.

45 Amishi P. Jha, "Mindfulness Can Improve Your Attention and Health," *Scientific American Mind* (March/April 2013).

46 Haidt, *The Happiness Hypothesis*; Siegel, *Mindsight*, 60–62.

47 Daniel Siegel, *The Mindful Brain: Reflection and Attunement in the Cultivation of Well-Being* (New York: WW Norton and Company, 2007), 5–15.

48 Siegel, *Mindsight*, 97–100.

49 Ibid., 86–7.

50 Center for Mindfulness in Medicine, Health Care and Society, University of Massachusetts Medical School, www.umassmed.edu/cfm.

51 Delores B. Lindsey, Richard S. Martinez, and Randall B. Lindsey, *Culturally Proficient Coaching, Supporting Educators to Create Equitable Schools* (Thousand Oaks, CA: Corwin Press, 2007).

CHAPTER 3. BIAS

1 Siri Carpenter, "Buried Prejudice," *Scientific American Mind* (April/May 2008), 33–39.

2 Project Implicit, "Frequently Asked Questions: #21 What is the difference between 'implicit' and 'automatic'?," www.implicit.harvard.edu.

3 D.M. Amodio and S.A. Mendoza, "Implicit Intergroup Bias: Cognitive, Affective, and Motivational Underpinnings," in *Handbook of Implicit Social Cognition*, ed. B. Gawronski and B.K. Payne (New York: Guilford, 2010), 353–74.

4 Shakil Choudhury, interview with Mahzarin Banaji, Toronto, May 10, 2013.

5 Banaji and Bhaskar, "Implicit Stereotypes and Memory," 140.

6 Hanson, *Buddha's Brain*, 6, 31–32.

7 Ibid., 70–73.

8 Timothy Wilson, *Strangers to Ourselves: Discovering the Adaptive Unconscious* (Belknap Press, 2004).

9 Ibid., 24.

10 David G. Myers, "The Powers and Perils of Intuition: Understanding the Nature of Our Gut Instincts," *Scientific American Mind* (June/July 2007), 26.

11 Ibid., 25–30.

12 Howard Ross, "Proven Strategies for Addressing Unconscious Bias in the Workplace," *Best Diversity Practices* (2008), 3.

13 Ibid.

14 Curtis D. Hardin and Mahzarin Banaji, "The Nature of Implicit Prejudice: Implications for Personal and Professional Policy," in *The Behavioral Foundations of Public Policy*, ed. Eldar Shafir (Princeton: Princeton University Press, 2012), 13–31.

15 Mahzarin Banaji and Anthony Greenwald, *Blind Spot: Hidden Biases of Good People* (New York: Delacorte Press, 2013).

16 Banaji and Bhaskar, "Implicit Stereotypes and Memory," 147.

17 Hardin and Banaji, "The Nature of Implicit Prejudice."

18 Banaji and Bhaskar, "Implicit Stereotypes and Memory," 142–45.

19 Project Implicit, "General Information," www.projectimplicit.net.

20 Hardin and Banaji, "The Nature of Implicit Prejudice."

21 Dora Capozza, Luca Andrighetto, Gian Antonio Di Bernardo, and Rosella Falvo, "Does Status Affect Intergroup Perceptions of Humanity?," *Group Process & Intergroup Relations* 15,3 (2012), 363–77.

22 Nosek, Banaji, and Greenwald, "Harvesting Implicit Group Attitudes and Beliefs," 101–115.

23 Hardin and Banaji, "The Nature of Implicit Prejudice."

24 Ibid.

25 Philip Oreopoulos, "Why Do Skilled Immigrants Struggle in the Labor Market? A Field Experiment with Six Thousand Résumés," University of British Columbia, National Bureau of Economic Research, and Canadian Institute for Advanced Research, June 2009.

26 Shankar Vedantam, "See No Bias," *The Washington Post*, www.washingtonpost.com, Jan. 23, 2005; also see the original study: Marianne Bertrand and Sendhil Mullainathan, "Are Emily and Greg More Employable Than Lakisha and Jamal? A Field Experiment on Labor Market Discrimination," University of Chicago Graduate School of Business, National Bureau of Economic Research, July 2003.

27 Alexandar R. Green et al., "Implicit Bias among Physicians and Its Prediction of Thrombolysis Decisions for Black and White Patients, *Journal of General Internal Medicine* 22,9 (2007), 1231–38.

28 Ibid.

29 Rebecca Hagey et al. (Centre for Equity in Health and Society), *Implementing Accountability for Equity and Ending Racial Backlash in Nursing: Accountability for Systemic Racism Must Be Guaranteed to Uphold Equal Rights in Society and Promote Equity in Health* (Toronto: Canadian Race Relations Foundation, 2005), xxi.

30 Jack Geiger, "Racial Stereotyping and Medicine: The Need for Cultural Competence," *Canadian Medical Association Journal* 164,12 (June 2001), 1699–1700.

31 Carpenter, "Buried Prejudice," 37–39.

32 Hardin and Banaji, "The Nature of Implicit Prejudice."

33 Banaji and Bhaskar, "Implicit Stereotypes and Memory," 147.

34 S. Alexander Haslam et al., "The Social Psychology of Success," *Scientific American Mind* (April/May 2008), 25–26.

35 Ibid.

36 Ibid.

37 Banaji and Greenwald, *Blind Spot*, 128–130.

38 Margaret Vogel, Alexandra Monesson, and Lisa S. Scott, "Building Biases in Infancy: The Influence of Race on Face and Voice Emotion Matching," *Developmental Science* 15,3 (May 2012), 359–72.

39 David J. Kelly, Paul C. Quinn, Alan M. Slater, Kang Lee, Liezhong Ge, and Olivier Pascalis, "The Other-Race Effect Develops During Infancy: Evidence of Perceptual Narrowing," *Psychological Science* 18,12 (Dec. 2007), 1084–89.

40 Banaji and Greenwald, *Blind Spot*, 128–130.

41 Leda Cosmides and John Tooby, "Evolutionary Psychology: New Perspectives on Cognition and Motivation," *Annual Review of Psychology* 64 (2013), 201–229.

42 D. Pietraszewski, L. Cosmides, and J. Tooby, "The Content of Our Cooperation, Not the Color of Our Skin: An Alliance Detection System Regulates Categorization by Coalition and Race, but Not Sex," *PLOS ONE* 9,2 (2014), e88534, doi:10.1371/journal.pone.0088534.

43 Myers, "The Powers and Perils of Intuition," 25–31.

44 Brandon Stewart and B. Keith Payne, "Bringing Automatic Stereotyping under Control: Implementation Intentions as Efficient Means of Thought Control," *Personality and Social Psychology Bulletin*, 34,10 (2008), 1332–45.

45 Carpenter, "Buried Prejudice," 37–38.

46 Choudhury, interview with Inzlicht, Sept. 17, 2012.

47 Carpenter, "Buried Prejudice," 38.

48 Ibid.

49 J. Kang and M. Banaji, "Fair Measures: A Behavioral Realist Revision of 'Affirmative Action,'" *California Law Review* 94 (2006), 1063–1118.

50 Hardin and Banaji, "The Nature of Implicit Prejudice."

51 Markus Brauer, Abdelatif Er-rafiy, Kerry Kawakami, and Curtis E. Phills, "Describing a Group in Positive Terms Reduces Prejudice Less Effectively Than Describing It in Positive and Negative Terms," *Journal of Experimental Social Psychology* 48 (2012), 757–61.

52 Brandon Stewart, "Bringing Automatic Stereotyping under Control: Implementation Intentions as Efficient Means of Thought Control," *Personality and Social Psychology Bulletin* 34,10 (Oct. 2008), 1334.

53 Brauer et al., "Describing a Group in Positive Terms."

54 Feng Sheng and Shihui Han, "Manipulations of Cognitive Strategies and Intergroup Relationships Reduce the Racial Bias in Empathic Neural Responses," *NeuroImage* 61 (2012), 786–97.

55 Lasana T. Harris and Susan T. Fiske, "Social Groups the Elicit Disgust Are Differentially Processed in the mPFC," *Social Cognitive Affective Neuroscience* 2 (2007), 45–51.

56 Patricia G. Devine, Patrick S. Forscher, Anthony J. Austin, and William T.L. Cox, "Long-Term Reduction in Implicit Race Bias: A Prejudice Habit-Breaking Intervention," *Journal of Experimental Social Psychology* 48 (2012), 1267–78.

57 Choudhury, interview with Inzlicht, Sept. 17, 2012.

58 Tiffany A. Ito and Bruce D. Bartholow, "The Neural Correlates of Race," *Trends in Cognitive Sciences* 13,12 (2009), 524–30.

59 Goleman, Boyatzis, and McKee, *Primal Leadership*, 46.

CHAPTER 4. TRIBES

1 Ontario Human Rights Commission (OHRC), "Preliminary Findings: Inquiry into Assaults on Asian Canadian Anglers," www.ohrc.on.ca, Dec. 2007.

2 Ibid.

3 Ibid.

4 Myers, "The Powers and Perils of Intuition," 31.

5 Norman Doidge, *The Brain That Changes Itself: Stories of Personal Triumph from the Frontiers of Brain Science* (New York: Penguin Books, 2007), 63–64.

6 Robert Jensen, *The Heart of Whiteness: Confronting Race, Racism and White Privilege* (San Francisco: City Lights Books, 2005), 14.

7 William B. Gudykunst, *Bridging Differences: Effective Intergroup Communications*, 3rd ed. (Thousand Oaks, CA: Sage Publications, 1998), 40–42.

8 Banaji and Greenwald, *Blind Spot*, 132–33.

9 Gudykunst, *Bridging Differences*, 40–48.

10 Ibid., 42.

11 Ibid., 14.

12 Jeanne Maglaty, "When Did Girls Start Wearing Pink?," *Smithsonian Magazine*, www.smithsonianmag.com, April 7, 2011.

13 Martin Smith, "I Cannot Shake Your Hand, Sir. I'm a Muslim and You're a Man," *The Daily Mail Online*, www.dailymail.co.uk, Jan. 20, 2007; Andy Levy-Ajzenkopf, "Deputy Mayor Offended by Handshake Snub," *The Canadian Jewish News*, www.cjnews.com, Feb. 14, 2008; Farooq Sulehria, "And Now the 'Handshake' Issue," *The News International*, http://thenews.jang.com.pk, March 18, 2010.

14 OHRC, "Preliminary Findings."

15 Ibid.

16 Ibid.

17 Shawn O. Utsey, Joseph G. Ponterotto, and Jerlym S. Porter, "Prejudice and Racism, Year 2008—Still Going Strong: Research on Reducing Prejudice with

Recommended Methodological Advances," *Journal of Counseling and Development* (June 22, 2008), 2–4.

18 Associated Press, "U.N.: Dozens of Muslims Massacred by Buddhists in Burma," www.cbsnews.com, Jan. 24, 2014.

19 BBC News Asia, "Pain of Pakistan's Outcast Ahmadis," www.bbc.com, Sept. 30, 2014.

20 PBS Frontline, "The Triumph of Evil: 100 Days of Slaughter: A Chronology of US/UN Actions," www.pbs.org, Jan. 1999.

21 Gudykunst, *Bridging Differences*, 31–32.

22 Goleman, Boyatzis, and McKee, *Primal Leadership*, 49–50.

23 C. Daniel Batson and Nadia Y. Ahmad, "Using Empathy to Improve Intergroup Attitudes and Relations," *Social Issues and Policy Review* 3,1 (2009), 141–77.

24 Siegel, *Mindsight*, 60–62.

CHAPTER 5. POWER

1 Jim Sidanius and Felicia Pratto, *Social Dominance: An Intergroup Theory of Hierarchy and Oppression* (New York: Cambridge University Press, 1999).

2 Ibid., 61.

3 Tina Lopez and Barb Thomas, *Dancing on Live Embers: Challenging Racism in Organizations* (Toronto: Between the Lines, 2006), 269.

4 Sidanius and Pratto, *Social Dominance*, 39–41.

5 Banaji and Greenwald, *Blind Spot*, 140–44.

6 Kirk Makin, "Of 100 New Federally Appointed Judges 98 Are White, Globe Finds," *The Globe and Mail* (Toronto), April 17, 2012.

7 Kirk Makin, "Minority Lawyers Demand Diversity among Appointed Judges," *The Globe and Mail* (Toronto), May 8, 2012.

8 Sidanius and Pratto, *Social Dominance*, 41.

9 Ibid., 129.

10 Ibid., 228–29.

11 Brian A. Nosek et al., "Pervasiveness and Correlates of Implicit Attitudes and Stereotypes," *European Review of Social Psychology* 1,52 (2007).

12 Sidanius and Pratto, *Social Dominance*, 229–31.

13 Brian A. Nosek, Mahzarin R. Banaji, and Anthony G. Greenwald, "Harvesting Implicit Group Attitudes and Beliefs from a Demonstration Web Site," *Group Dynamics: Theory, Research, and Practice* 6,1 (2002), 101–115.

14 Sidanius and Pratto, *Social Dominance*, 229–31.

15 Edward Selby et al., "Self Sabotage: The Enemy Within," *Psychology Today*, www. psychologytoday.com, Sept. 2, 2011.

16 "Javier Espinoza: Turning Pain into Power" in *5 Brave Personal Stories of Domestic Abuse*, TED: Ideas Worth Spreading, http://blog.ted.com, Jan. 25, 2013.

17 Sidanius and Pratto, *Social Dominance*, 259.

18 Ibid., 248–49.

19 Ibid.

20 Ibid., 256–62.

21 Rob Kunzia, "Racism in Schools: Unintentional but No Less Damaging," *Pacific Standard*, www.psmag.com, April 8, 2009.

22 Ontario Human Rights Commission, "Human Rights Settlement Reached with Ministry of Education," 2005.

23 Sidanius and Pratto, *Social Dominance*, 103–125.

24 Ibid., 106; Lydia Saad, "Black-White Educational Opportunities Widely Seen as Equal," *Gallup*, www.gallup.com, July 2, 2007; Frank Newport, "Little 'Obama Effect' on Views about Race Relations," *Gallup*, Oct. 29, 2009.

25 Knowledge@Wharton, "To Increase Charitable Donations, Appeal to the Heart— Not the Head," Wharton School of the University of Pennsylvania, http://knowledge. wharton.upenn.edu, 2007.

26 Associated Press, "Obama Quits Church after Controversy," *USA Today*, http://usatoday.com, June 1, 2008.

27 Hannity and Colmes, "Obama's Pastor: Rev. Jeremiah Wright," Fox News, transcript, www.foxnews.com, March 1, 2007.

28 Chris Dudley, "Video: Alamogordo Tea Party Protestors Pack Heat," *The New Mexico Independent*, Feb. 1, 2010.

29 Lila Shapiro, "Man Carrying Semi-automatic Assault Rifle and Pistol outside Obama Event," *Huffington Post*, www.huffingtonpost.com, Sept. 17, 2009.

30 "Missouri Approves Concealed Guns at School and Open Carry in Public," *The Guardian*, www.theguardian.com, Sept. 11, 2014.

CHAPTER 6. POWER PART 2

1 The Process Work approach to rank and power comes from the work of Arnold Mindell, author of *The Deep Democracy of Open Forums* (Hampton Roads, 2002) and *Sitting in the Fire* (Deep Democracy Exchange, 2014).

2 Kate Allen, "Suspension Lengthened for Coach Who Opposed Slur," *Toronto Star*, www.thestar.com, Dec. 17, 2010.

3 Molly Hayes, "Video: Hamilton Bigotry 'Experiment' Ends with·a Punch," *The Hamilton Spectator*, www.thespec.com, Oct. 30, 2014.

4 Shakil Choudhury, interview with Julie Diamond, July 2, 2014.

5 Ibid.

6 Goleman, Boyatzis, and McKee, *Primal Leadership*, 51–52.

7 Choudhury, interview with Diamond, July 2, 2014.

8 Jon Henly, "I Feel Terribly Guilty," *The Guardian*, www.guardian.com, Nov. 4, 2004.

CHAPTER 7. DEEP DIVERSITY

1 Asubpeeschoseewagong First Nation, www.grassynarrows.ca.

2 "Mercury Poisoning Effects Continue at Grassy Narrows," CBC News, www.cbc.ca, June 4, 2012.

3 Jody Porter, "'Longest Running' First Nations Blockade Continues," CBC News, www.cbc.ca, Dec. 3, 2012.

4 Stephen M. Southwick and Dennis S. Charney, "Ready for Anything," *Scientific American Mind* (July/Aug. 2013), 32–41.

5 Haidt, *The Happiness Hypothesis*, 146–49.

6 The details of Francine's story and the Oka crisis are well documented in Loreen Pindera, "A Sister's Grief Bridges a Cultural Divide: Revisiting the Oka Standoff," CBC News, www.cbc.ca, July 8, 2010; and Loreen Pindera, "Bringing Down the Barricades," originally aired on CBC Radio's *C'est la Vie* with Bernard St. Laurent in June 2010.

7 Ingrid Peritz, "Sister of Slain Officer at Oka Makes Peace with Mohawks," *The Globe and Mail*, www.theglobeandmail.com, July 4, 2010.

8 Ibid.

9 Pindera, "A Sister's Grief."

10 Ibid.

11 Ibid.

12 Pindera, "Bringing Down the Barricades."

13 Pindera, "A Sister's Grief."

14 Pindera, "Bringing Down the Barricades."

15 Steve Pinker and Andrew Mack, "The World Is Not Falling Apart," *Slate*, www.slate.com, Dec. 22, 2014.

16· Ann Curry, "Dalai Lama: Humanity Is Getting Better—Video," *Today Show*, www.today.com, May 20, 2010.

INDEX